School Is Out

How to Survive and Thrive Financially

Dominique Trapp

Acknowledgments

This book is a lifelong goal of mine that couldn't have been achieved without the support of my extraordinary wife, Dorothy. To my project team members Zion, Dion, and Ricardo, your contributions were invaluable and instrumental in the success of our project.

I dedicate this book to my sons, Ethan, and Marcellus. Hopefully, this book serves as a reminder of what preparation, discipline and perseverance can accomplish.

Contents

Preface

There are children who are unfortunate in their circumstances and upbringing. They only know what is taught at home, in their community, and at school. I feel an obligation to give back to the youth, so they can take advantage of knowledge and information that I wish I was exposed to at their age. I find myself gravitating toward educating the youth on financial principles and education, given the impact finance can have on our lives.

Over the years, I have attempted to share financial skills, knowledge, and experiences with my younger relatives and now children. From a near-sighted perspective, my actions could be considered notable, but far-sighted, those same actions could be perceived as selfish since I only share with my family. I always wanted to change the latter and pay it forward to all. Whether a youth's financial aspiration is modest or ambitious, they deserve the ability to understand and manage their personal finances effectively. This includes knowledge about budgeting, saving, investing, and understanding financial risks and opportunities. I hope this book will inspire them, challenge them, and equip them with the tools and knowledge they need to achieve their financial dreams.

Introduction

The U.S. has a financial literacy problem. The root cause traces back to the U.S. education system which does not teach our kids how money, finance, and credit work. As of 2023:

- 75% of American teens lack confidence in their knowledge of personal finance.[1]
- 25% of Americans say they don't have anyone they can ask for trusted financial guidance.[1]

These kids, now young adults, enter adulthood oblivious to the problem until after making a money, finance, or credit mistake. These same young adults may never learn what to do with their money, finance, and credit, thus passing down this lack of knowledge and behavioral patterns to the next generation of kids. This problem drove me to write this book, so young adults can avoid unnecessary financial mistakes, teenagers can have a source of making sound financial decisions and adults can improve their financial circumstances. Eliminate the formulas, financial jargon, and acronyms, you'll realize managing your finances is simple math and common sense. This book is broken down into three segments: Money, Finance and Credit. Each segment contains chapters focused on key areas of the subject matter. You are eased into the book with Chapter 1, which covers your paystub attributes and explains how to calculate hourly pay from gross annual salary, and vice versa. The first paycheck is the beginning of teenagers' financial journey and the start of misguided financial habits.

In Chapter 2, we discuss the mantra "Pay Yourself First" and ways to take action such as a 401k and Individual Retirement Account (IRA). After you have paid yourself first, you'll learn it is not what you make, but what you keep in Chapter 3, which entails the purpose of saving and checking accounts, the importance of a spending plan, the accumulation of emergency savings as well as options to receive income on your savings. You're then shown how to open an account to purchase U.S. Treasury Bills and Certificate of Deposits (CDs). I would be remiss not to inform you about investment avenues ROTH IRA and Personal Brokerage Account.

Rounding out the last chapter in the money segment, Chapter 4, we introduce two traits: financial discipline and delayed gratification. Equipping yourself with financial knowledge to make a difference in your life serves no purpose without the mental attitude to consistently follow through on your financial plan. Our economy and society are constructed to make you a consumer of experiences and goods consciously and subconsciously; thus, the reason 70% of the U.S. economy is dependent on your (consumer) spending. If gone unchecked, you may find yourself in a desperate need to obtain an amount of income to keep up with your peers and social groups. Worst case scenario, your self-worth is defined by the amount of income you earn. Idealizing huge houses, fancy cars and designer clothes is the invisible cheese dangling in front of the rat trap. Once trapped, you are stuck working endlessly to pay for these idealized items.

The next segment, Finance, opens with you learning about assets and liabilities in Chapter 5. Since assets lead to income generation, value appreciation and wealth accumulation, while liabilities have the opposite effect. We will dive deeper into the realm of liabilities (debt) in the following chapters by showing you how to:

1.   Determine a loan monthly payment.
2.   Determine a loan interest rate based on the monthly payment.
3.   Determine the credit card balance interest for the month.
4.   Determine a line of credit interest for the month.

Before your mind starts racing about the math involved in the topics just mentioned, take a breath. We will use a free financial calculator to enter values into specific fields. The free financial calculator is downloadable from your cell phone's Apple Store or Play Store. As a result of these chapter lessons, you can avoid deceitful monthly loan payments from car dealerships and lenders. Chapter 8 covers the strategies and benefits of eliminating debt and leveraging liabilities for income and value creation. In Chapter 9, you learn how inflation plays a factor in your finances and cost of living. We then cover the impact of inflation on nominal and real rates. Chapter 10 teaches you about compounding interest, the rule of 72 and the present value (future value) of money. To emphasize the point of each method, we'll walk through real-life scenarios.

In the last segment, Credit, you'll learn ways to establish credit as well as how your credit score (FICO score) is determined in Chapter 10. You're also introduced to websites for tracking your credit score and obtaining a free annual credit report. Before concluding the last chapter, we'll cover the benefits of good credit and the best practices for maintaining good credit. Throughout the chapters, there are quick exercises for each topic. At the end of each chapter, a small test is given to reassure your confidence in the subject. Your journey to becoming financially literate (savvy) doesn't stop at the end of this book; therefore, I recommend a few books to keep you moving forward and provide words of encouragement in my final thoughts. I hope you are as excited as I am to get started.

Chapter 1

Pay Stub Details: Why They Matter and How to Understand Them

You cannot prevail with understanding your money without understanding your pay stub. Let's assume you're Joe Doe making $15 an hour at a retail shop working 40 hours per week (8 hours x 5 Days). On payday, you either receive a check along with the pay stub or an electronic deposit with online access to the pay stub. Exhibit 1.1 is the first section of your paystub, including the company (employer) name and address as well as your name and address.

Company: Snappy Frank's	Employee: Joe Doe
Company Address: 1245 Eastway BLVD	Employee Address: 133 Lake DR
Charlotte, NC 28202	Charlotte, NC 28269

Name	Employee ID	Pay Period Begin	Pay Period End	Pay Date (Check Date)	Pay Frequency
Joe Doe	1254154	6/4/2023	6/17/2023	6/23/2023	Bi-Weekly

Rate	Current Hours	YTD Hours	Current Earnings	YTD Earnings
15.00	80.00	320.00	1,200.00	4,800.00

Exhibit 1.1 First Section of Your Pay Stub

That same section of the pay stub has the following details:

- Employee ID – identification number assigned to you by your employer
- Pay Period Begin – pay period start date
- Pay Period End – pay period end date
- Pay Date (Check Date) – date your paycheck is issued or electronically deposited
- Pay Frequency – how often you are paid
- Rate – hourly pay rate
- Current Hours – number of hours worked in the pay period
- YTD Hours – year-to-date hours worked so far
- Current Earnings – money made during the pay period
- YTD Earnings – year-to-date money made

Notice the pay frequency is bi-weekly. Another common pay frequency is semi-annually, meaning payday is on the 15th and 30th (31st) of each month. The next section of your pay stub contains Employee Taxes, Pre-Tax Deductions and After-Tax Deductions. Exhibit 1.2 is a view of your Snappy Frank's pay stub employee taxes with the current column representing your taxes for the pay period. The YTD column represents the sum of each employee tax paid since the beginning of the year.

Employee Taxes

Description	Current	YTD
Social Security (OASDI)	74.40	297.60
Medicare	17.40	69.60
Federal Withholdings	71.64	286.56
State Taxes - NC	33.96	135.84
Total (Taxes)		

Exhibit 1.2 Snappy Frank's Pay Stub Employee Taxes

Let's walk through each employee tax, starting with Social Security (OASD), which is a government program where you pay a percentage of your gross pay per period to the program until you reach retirement age. That percentage is 6.20% as of 2023. Once you reach retirement age and apply to receive social security income, officially named Supplement Security Income, the program provides you money monthly. As of 2023, the earliest you can receive supplement security income is age 62, but there is a catch. You won't receive the full monthly income amount at that age. The rationale for setting the recipient age to 62 is influenced by three factors: life expectancy, financial needs, and workforce considerations. The reason behind the reduction of the full monthly income amount starting at age 62 isn't quite clear, but the decision disincentives program participates from starting the supplement security payments at that age. If you're interested in additional information on social security income and benefits, please visit the ssa.gov website.[2]

Medicare is another government program but for health insurance. The program provides healthcare coverage for people aged 65 and older, certain younger people with disabilities as well as other circumstances. To sustain the program funding, you pay 1.45% of your gross pay as of 2023.

Next up is Federal Withholding, aka Uncle Sam's federal taxes. The government determines the amount of money that you paid for federal withholding using two factors:

1. The amount of money you earn.
2. The information that you provide on your W-4 form, which indicates your tax status.

The two factors mentioned aren't much to determine the percentage of money deducted from your pay stub; however, there are plenty of free tools that calculate your pay period employee taxes. One of the tools is the website www.paycheckcity.com, which has an hourly calculator and a salary calculator.

Take a moment to use the salary calculator to determine your federal withholding based on your Snappy Frank's pay stub. Follow the instructions below:

1. Go to www.paycheckcity.com.
2. On the home screen's horizontal bar, click on the **FREE CALCULATORS.**
3. In the FREE CALCULATORS screen, click on the **Salary Calculator** icon or link.
4. In the Salary Calculator screen, select the **State** that you work in. Recall, you work in the state of North Carolina (NC) per your pay stub information.
5. Next, select the **Check Date**, which is your pay period date of 6-23-2023.
6. In the calculator Earnings section, enter the Current Earnings amount (Gross Pay Amount) from your pay stub in the **Gross Pay field**. E.g. $1,200.
7. Select Pay Per Period in the **Gross Pay Method** field.
8. Skip entering a value in the **Gross Pay YTD** field.
9. In the **Pay Frequency** field, select bi-weekly.
10. In the Federal Taxes section of the calculator, select Single or Married filing separately in the **Federal Filing Status** field, given that you are single at this point.
11. Since you do not have dependents, deductions or other income, skip the rest of the Federal Taxes section as well as North Carolina State and Local Taxes section.
12. Click on the **Calculate** button.

The calculator results are broken down by gross pay, employee taxes including the federal withholding and net pay. The federal withholding amount is an estimation; thus, a small variance is probable. Compare the calculator's federal withholding amount in Exhibit 1.4 to your Snappy Frank's pay stub federal withholding amount.

Paycheck Results	
Gross Pay	$1,200.00
Federal Withholding	$71.62
Social Security	$74.40
Medicare	$17.40
State Withholding	$34.00
Take Home Pay	
Net Pay	$1,002.58

Exhibit 1.4 Pay Stub Results[4]

Tip: *Salary (Hourly) Calculator tool is great for finding your take home pay (net pay) when considering a job offer pay.*

You may have noticed the State Withholding amount displayed in the calculator results in Exhibit 1.4. Uncle Sam collects again from you with a second tax—the State Withholding. There are options available if you desire not to pay state income tax. Here are places where there is no state income tax: Alaska, Florida, Nevada, South Dakota, Tennessee, Texas, Washington or Wyoming.

While California may be the place where dreams come true, those dreams come with a hefty price ticket. California has the highest state income tax at 13.3% as of 2022. The remaining top five states with high state income tax are Hawaii at 11%, New Jersey at 10.75%, Oregon at 9.9% and Minnesota at 9.85%.[4] Your work and living location are significant factors that impact your money due to state income tax differences, amongst other things. Be aware of this when you're making your work and living location choice.

Quick Exercise 1.1

If you are currently working, use the salary calculator tool to calculate your most recent pay stub. Observe your actual pay stub results vs. the calculator pay stub results. If you are not currently working, use the salary calculator tool to calculate the bi-weekly gross pay of $1,200 working in the state of New York with the tax status as single. Is the New York state withholding amount higher or lower than your Snappy's Franks pay stub amount (North Carolina)?

Pre-Tax Deductions are line items from benefits offered by your employer. After enrolling in the benefits, you are required to pay a premium per pay period. The premiums are paid from your gross pay before your gross pay is taxed by Uncle Sam (federal and state withholdings). Exhibit 1.5 is the section of your Snappy's Franks pay stub Pre-Tax Deductions.

Pre-Tax Deductions

Description	Current	YTD
Pre-tax 401(k)	72.00	288.00
Dental Premium (Pre Tax)	6.30	25.20
Vision Premium (Pre-Tax)	2.34	9.36
Medical Premium (Pre-Tax)	65.00	260.00
Total (Pre-Tax Deductions)	145.64	582.56

Exhibit 1.5 Pay Stub Pre-Tax Deductions

The most common benefits offered by your employer are medical insurance, dental insurance, vision insurance and 401K. Medical insurance covers doctor visits, prescription drugs, surgeries, etc. Dental insurance includes routine teeth cleanings, fillings, root canals, etc. Vision insurance covers routine eye appointments, lenses, and frames for glasses. Less self-explanatory is the 401k, which allows you to invest a portion of your gross pay for your retirement. More to come on a 401k in the next chapter!

There are some benefits offered by your employer where the premium is paid after Uncle Sam's taxes; hence, the name After-Tax Deductions. An example of an after-tax deduction benefit is life insurance, which pays a lump sum of money to a person (beneficiary) when someone else dies who is covered by the plan.

In your Snappy's Franks pay stub, Exhibit 1.6, you're enrolled into your employer's optional term life insurance plan.

After- Tax Deductions

Description	Current	YTD
Optional Term Life (Post Tax)	5.00	20.00
Total (After-Tax Deductions	5.00	20.00

Exhibit 1.6 Pay Stub After-Tax Deductions

At the bottom of your pay stub is a summary for the current and YTD periods. Your net pay is included in the pay summary. In this case, your Snappy's Franks net pay is $851.96 for the pay period. See Exhibit 1.7 Pay Stub Summary.

Pay Summary

	Gross Pay	Pre-Tax Deductions	Employee Taxes	After Tax Deductions	Net Pay
Current	1,200.00	145.64	197.40	5.00	851.96
YTD	4,800.00	582.56	789.60	20.00	3,407.84

Exhibit 1.7 Pay Stub Summary

Calculation of Hourly Pay to Gross Annual Salary

In school, you learned to annualize an amount by multiplying the monthly amount by 12, since there are 12 months in a year. For example, to annualize a monthly payment of $5,000, you multiply the monthly payment by 12 to arrive at $60,000. However, the approach is wrong when annualizing your gross annual salary. For instance, your bi-weekly gross pay is $2,500, so you multiply $2,500 by two to arrive at your monthly pay of $5,000. You then multiply $5,000 by 12 to arrive at $60,000 for your gross annual salary. That is wrong!

Let's assume your hourly pay is $31.25. You work 40 hours a week; therefore, your weekly gross pay amount is $1,250. To determine your gross annual salary, you multiply $1,250 by 52, since there are 52 weeks in a year. Your gross annual salary is $65,000, not $60,000.

Gross Annual Salary = Weekly Gross Pay Amount x 52

Weekly Gross Pay = Hourly Pay x Number of Hours Worked in a Week

Here is a scenario that emphasizes the importance. You interviewed for a job and the employer decided you are the best fit. The employer offered you $20 an hour. You expected the offer to be a gross annual salary of $40,000, but you calculated the $20 an hour to $38,400. The correct annualized amount is $41,600, which is above your expected gross annual salary amount. Since you are unaware of the calculation error, you make the following decisions:

1. Decline the job since the job offer does not meet your salary requirement of $40,000.
2. Counter the offer that results in no change; therefore, you have a sour attitude toward the offer. You accept the offer since it's your only job offer.

Decision # 1 leaves you with no job; thus, you are back to the grind of applying, waiting, and interviewing for a job. Decision # 2 causes you to have a bitter attitude going into the job, compromising your effort and first impression; consequently, unknown opportunities are lost. But what if you were aware of the calculation error and you realized the $20 an hour exceeded your salary expectation? Decision # 3: you are ecstatic about the job, so you accept the offer; consequently, the following outcomes happen:

1. You save or invest the $1,600 that exceeds your salary requirement of $40,000.
2. Your enthusiasm for the job translates to incredible effort and a remarkable first impression; as a result, unknown opportunities come your way.

As you can see, a simple calculation error can lead to poor decisions and emotions that railroad your present and future income (money).

Quick Exercise 1.2

Determine the gross annual salary of $65 an hour working 40 hours a week.

Calculation of Gross Annual Salary to Hourly Pay

The same flaw in calculating the hourly pay to gross annual salary is found when calculating the gross annual salary to hourly pay. For instance, your gross annual salary is $75,000. Using your school math, you divide $75,000 by 12 months to arrive at your monthly pay of $6,250. You then divide 6,250 by 4 weeks to arrive at your weekly pay of $1,562.50. Lastly, you divide $1,562.40 by 40 hours to arrive at $39.06 per hour. While the approach is solid mathematically, the outcome is wrong. The correct hourly amount is determined by dividing $75,000 by 52 weeks to arrive at your weekly pay of $1,442.31. Then divide $1,442.31 by 40 hours to arrive at 36.06 per hour. As a result, the correct amount is less than $3 of the incorrect amount.

Quick Exercise 1.3

Determine the hourly pay for a gross annual salary of $85,000 working 40 hours a week.

When you're in a salary profession, your hourly pay is dictated by the number of hours worked per week. So far, we assume the work week is 40 hours; however, most high-paying salary professionals work more than 40 hours per week. Perhaps your gross annual salary is $100,000, but you work 60 hours a week. Your hourly pay of $32.05 is equivalent to a gross annual salary of $66,664 on a 40-hour per week basis. In this case, the value of your gross annual salary significantly declines due to the extensive hours worked. Keep this in mind when you are seeking a high-income professional career since the value of free time tends to go undervalued until the free time is desired or needed. You could find yourself contemplating your beloved career (lifestyle) vs. your desperately needed free time for your mental health or family.

Quick Exercise 1.4

Which gross annual salary option represents the best hourly pay value?

a. $200,000 working 65 hours a week
b. $150,000 working 50 hours a week
c. $100,000 working 40 hours a week

Quick Exercise Answers

1.   If you are not currently working, the answer is yes

2. $135,200

$65 (Pay Per Hours) x 40 (Work Hours in a Week) x 52 (52 Weeks in a Year)

3. $40.86

$85,000 (Salary Offer) ÷ 52 (52 Weeks in a Year) ÷ 40 (40 Work Hours in a Week) = $40.86

3.   A ($200,000 working 65 hours a week)

Chapter Test

1. Select a Pre-Tax Deduction item:
    a. Federal Withholding
    b. Life Insurance
    c. Medical Insurance
    d. Social Security (OASDI)
2. Select a purpose of Medicare:
   a. To provide healthcare to all U.S. citizens
   b. To provide healthcare to senior citizens age 65 and older
   c. To provide medicine vouchers at 15% discount
   d. To combat homelessness
3. Every state in the U.S. has state withholding tax (income tax).
    a. True
    b. False
4. If you pay your federal withholding tax, you do not have to pay your state withholding tax.
    a. True
    b. False
5. Select an After-Tax Deduction item:
    a. 401k
    b. Vision Insurance
    c. Life Insurance
6. Jake is offered a salary of $120,000 working 40 hours a week. Jake's hourly pay requirement is $50.00. Does the salary offer of $120,000 meet Jake's hourly pay requirement?
7. Mary has two job offers. The first offer pays $35 an hour working 45 hours a week. The second offer pays $45 an hour working 38 hours a week. Which offer has the highest paying gross annual salary?

Chapter Test Answers

1. C (Medical Insurance)
2. B (To provide healthcare to senior citizens age 65 and older)
3. B (False)
4. B (False)
5. C (Life Insurance)
6. Yes

$120,000 (Salary Offer) ÷ 52 (52 Weeks in a Year) ÷ 40 (40 Work Hours in a Week) = $57.69, which is greater than $50

7. Offer pays $45 an hour working 38 hours a week

$45 (Pay Per Hours) x 38 (Work Hours in a Week) x 52 (52 Weeks in a Year) = $88,920 is greater than

$35 (Pay Per Hours) x 45 (Work Hours in a Week) x 52 (52 Weeks in a Year) = $81,900

Chapter 2

Pay Yourself First

As you establish yourself into adulthood, you will find yourself in fear of losing what you have worked so hard to obtain: your car and house (or apartment). Thus, you will have a religious commitment to make on-time payments for your car loan and mortgage (or rent). Prioritize this same level of commitment by paying yourself first, since it is you who is performing at your job daily despite fighting through work challenges and life obligations. The first beneficiary of your paycheck ought to be you, not the government or the bill collector. Failing to pay yourself first has an economic effect on your money. Let me explain how.

As you learned in Chapter 1, before employee taxes are deducted from your gross pay, pre-tax deductions are deducted first. Here is the opportunity to pay yourself first by allocating a percentage of your gross pay to your 401k. The system is designed to allow businesses to deduct their expenses before paying taxes thus allowing businesses to take care of themselves first before paying the government. The allocation of money to a 401k has the same advantage but for people. A 401k presents the opportunity to invest your money before it is taxed. Your employer must offer a 401k program in order for you to have one.

Once you have met the employment period with your employer, your employer matches a percentage of your gross pay that you contribute to your 401k. For example, your employer matches 6% of your gross pay to your 401k after your first year of employment.

Your Contribution: Gross Pay $1,200 x 401k Match Rate of 6%
= $72

Your Employer Contribution: Gross Pay $1,200 x 401k Match Rate 6% = $72

Your Total 401k Contribution for the Pay Period: $144

Remember: You must contribute a percentage of your gross pay to your 401K for your employer to contribute the same percentage.

Quick Exercise 2.1

What is the total contribution amount when the gross pay amount is $3,000, the contribution percentage is 3% and the employer is matching the contribution percentage?

Your employer's contribution to your 401k is free money; hence, the economic effect mentioned earlier. For the following reasons, taking advantage of this free money aligns with your best interest:

1. Your pay period contribution doubles. E.g., your pay period contribution doubled from $72 to $144. There is no easier way to double your money than to contribute the money to your

401K. The decision does not involve you taking a business risk or betting your money.

2. There is a good chance that your employer does not offer a pension plan; therefore, your employer's investment toward your retirement is their 401k contributions. As of 2021, 3% of workers for private companies have access to a pension plan known as a defined benefit plan.[5]

3. The amount of money in your 401k can accumulate faster. As you'll learn in Chapter 8, time can be your best friend or worst enemy.

4. You're less reliant on the government's social security program, which has become a political target for reduction and elimination.

5. The money in your 401k is not taxed as the money increases in value from the accumulation of interest, dividends, and capital gains.

These advantages do come with strings attached. Once you contribute money to your 401k, there is a 10% penalty to withdraw the money before the age of 59 ½, unless your withdrawal meets the following conditions:[6]

1. Death
2. Disability
3. First-time homebuyer
4. Income purposes
5. Health insurance premiums
6. Higher education expense
7. If you owe the IRS
8. Unreimbursed medical bills

Let's say you haven't met the age requirement yet but decide to withdraw $30,000 from your 401k to purchase a boat. Since your withdrawal reason does not qualify for the 10% penalty exception, $3,000 is deducted from your 401k balance as an early withdrawal penalty. Your 401k balance decreases by $33,000 in total. From my perspective, the first-time home buyer, the higher education expense nor the IRS condition justify the decision to sacrifice a portion of your future retirement for a current problem.

The system allows these exceptions as a quick fix to plug the financial education gap that results in workers falling behind on saving for buying a home or paying for their kids' college education. Chapter 3 provides the solution to the issue of falling behind on your savings.

Quick Exercise 2.2

You decide to withdraw $12,000 from your 401k to purchase an engagement ring. Does the engagement ring withdrawal reason qualify for the withdrawal penalty exception? If so, what is the withdrawn penalty dollar amount?

When you do choose to withdraw money from your 401k during retirement, you must pay income taxes on the withdrawn amount as if it is working income. While the decision to pay your first seems like a no-brainer, you may find yourself struggling to apply the principle. One of the reasons for this is affordability. If you are already in the workforce, working full time, you may be thinking, "I cannot afford to contribute to my 401k, since the decision reduces the amount of money left in my paycheck; as a result, I have less money to pay for my living expenses."

I encourage you to reconsider this perspective given that the money lost from your employer's contribution can't be recovered. The time lost for your contributions and your employer's contributions to produce interest, dividends, and capital gains is insurmountable. The financially literate (savvy) action is to reduce your monthly living expenses, which is easier said than done, in some people's eyes, but is achievable. You will learn how in Chapter 3.

Another reason you may be struggling to apply the principle is short-sightedness. You may feel that you have time to pay yourself first later, due to your young age or confidence to make up the lost contribution with higher contribution amounts as your income increases. The scientific laws of compounding interest prove neither makes up for the lost time. For young adults entering the workforce, you are now aware of the issue; therefore, you can avoid incurring a level of monthly living expenses that is difficult to eliminate or reduce. Better yet, you can set your contribution percentage to your 401k early before creating these living expenses. Check out the difference in accumulated 401k balances in five years due to the one-year delay of contribution in Exhibit 2.1.

Exhibit 2.1 Assumptions:

- Bi-weekly gross pay is $1,200
- Bi-weekly gross pay does not increase over the five-year period
- 401k contribution is 6% of gross pay
- Employer matches 401k contribution at 6% after one year

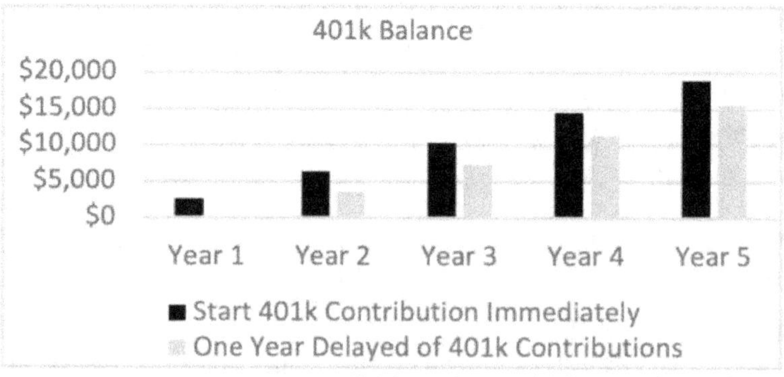

Exhibit 2.1 Impact of Delay in 401k Contribution

The difference becomes even larger as time passes forward; thus, the one-year delayed of 401k contributions never catches up to the start 401k contribution immediately. To make the point, see the significant difference when the 401k contributions are delayed by three years in Exhibit 2.2.

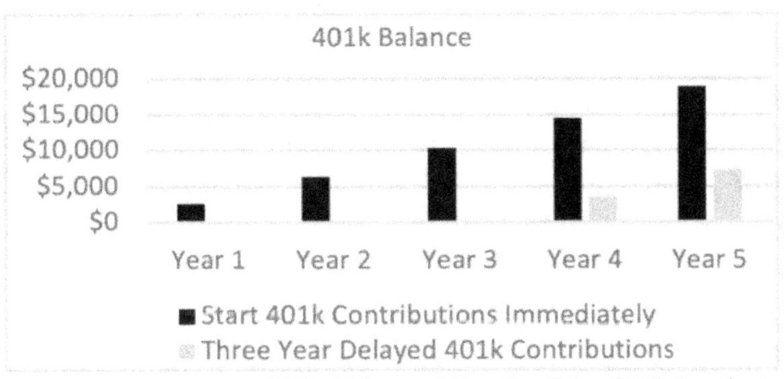

Exhibit 2.2 Impact of Three Year Delay of 401k Contribution

The three-year delayed 401k contributions fall short of the start 401k contributions immediately by at least 2.58 times.

IRA

There are circumstances where you are not eligible for your employer's 401k program, or your employer does not offer a 401k program. Don't sweat it. You still can pay yourself first by opening an Individual Retirement Account (IRA). An IRA allows you to contribute a portion of your gross pay, like a 401k, except your employer does not contribute money to an IRA. You are the sole contributor. An IRA has the same advantage as a 401k, which allows money in the account to increase tax-free; thus, you only pay taxes on the money when withdrawn. Some of the pros of IRA compared to a 401k are as follows:

1. The purchase of individual stocks in an IRA.

2. An IRA provider, also known as a brokerage service, has a vast amount of investment options to choose from. In the case of a 401k, your employer determines the investment options available in the program by the brokerage service. While the employer may have good intentions for limiting the number of investment options within the program, those good intentions can be a disservice to you.

As with the 401k, you will incur a 10% withdrawal penalty when money is withdrawn from an IRA account before the age of 59 ½. Below are withdrawal penalty exceptions for an IRA:[7]

1. Birth or adoption expenses
2. Death
3. Disability
4. Domestic Abuse
5. Emergency Personal Expense
6. First-time homebuyer
7. Income purposes
8. Health insurance premiums
9. Higher education expense
10. If you owe the IRS
11. Periodic payments
12. Qualified Disaster
13. Reservist IRA distribution
14. Unreimbursed medical bills

Quick Exercise 2.3

Your employer can contribute to your IRA:

a. True

b. False

Quick Exercise Answers

1. $180

    $3,000 (Gross Pay) x .06 (Your Contribution of 3% plus Employe Contribution of 3% Percentage)

2. No ($1,200)

    $12,000 (Withdraw Amount) x .10 (Withdraw Penalty)

3. B (False)

Chapter Test

1. A 401k and IRA allow you to pay yourself first before paying government and bill collectors.
    a. True
    b. False
2. What is a 401k contribution:
    a. Allocation of money after taxes to a 401k
    b. A charitable donation after taxes
    c. Allocation of money before taxes to a 401k
    d. A charitable donation before taxes
3. What is the contribution amount when the gross pay amount is $5,000, the contribution percentage is 5% and the employer is not matching the contribution percentage?
4. Select a withdrawn reason that qualifies for 401k withdrawn penalty exception:
    a. Purchase of a car
    b. Investment in non-profit business
    c. A loan to your parents
    d. Higher education expense
5. You have to pay income tax on money withdrawn from a 401k or an IRA.
    a. True
    b. False
6. You're 35 years old and withdrew $50,000 from your IRA to purchase a barbershop. What is the withdrawal penalty amount?

Chapter Test Answers

1. A (True)

2. C (Allocation of money before taxes to a 401k)

3. $250

   $5,000 (Gross Pay) x .05 (Percentage of Contribution)

4. D (Higher Education Expense)

5. A (True)

6. $5,000

   $50,000 (Withdraw Amount) x .10 (Withdraw Penalty)

Chapter 3

Income: It's Not What You Make But What You Keep

A business is not valued on how much revenue it generates, but how much revenue it keeps and profits. For a business to keep its revenue, a deliberate effort is made to keep its expenses low. The same approach can't be said about people's income. Why is that? I suspect the following reasons:

1. A lack of knowledge of the approach.
2. The decision to only save income after paying expenses (bills) and spending on desires.
3. The decision to not save income at all.
4. A substantially low income.

When the reason is a substantially low income, the only solution is to find opportunities to increase your income whether it is a new job, second job, gig job, or side hustle. There is a remedy to the other reasons. Reverse engineer the decision to save income after paying expenses and desired spending. To do this, set a monthly savings amount before considering anything else with your income. Once the monthly savings amount is set, the remaining income can pay for your bills and desires within the month. If you don't have enough income to pay for your bills, then review each bill for reduction or elimination. This action must occur at least once a year. Preferably, this action ought to occur on a semi-annual basis.

You may be asking yourself, what's an adequate amount of money to save monthly? The answer depends on your income and preference. A few financial resources recommend allocating 20% of your income to your savings. If you care to know, I save an average of 33% of my income. In the most recent years, that percentage has increased to 43%. Some people elect to be frugal; thus, saving an extremely high percentage of their income. Their decision may result in a drastic lifestyle change such as canceling their apartment lease and living in a mobile camper. Other people may decide to increase their income with a new job, second job, or side hustle instead of cutting back on expenses and desires. With that said, let's assume the decisions below are yours as you review your spending plan approaches, Exhibit 3.1.

A. Old approach—decide to save personal income after paying expenses and spending on desires.
B. New approach—decide to set saving amount first before paying expenses and spending on desires.
C. New approach—decide to increase personal income and leave expenses unchanged.

A		B		C	
Monthly Net Pay	3,300	Monthly Net Pay	3,300	Monthly Net Pay	4,050
Rent	1,400	Rent	900	Rent	1,400
Car Payment	350	Car Payment	350	Car Payment	350
Grocery	200	Grocery	200	Grocery	200
Student Loan	150	Student Loan	150	Student Loan	150
Cable	160	Cable Netflix	18	Cable	160
Cell phone	80	Cell phone	80	Cell phone	80
Utilities	60	Utilities	60	Utilities	60
Car Insurance	120	Car Insurance	70	Car Insurance	120
Renter Insurance	30	Renter Insurance	30	Renter Insurance	30
Internet	70	Internet	70	Internet	70
Desires	600	Desires	712	Desires	600
Saving	80	Saving	660	Saving	830

Exhibit 3.1 Spending Plan Approaches

Decision A spending plan is only saving $80 a month. Decision B spending plan applies the approach to set the monthly saving amount first, in this case to 20% of the monthly income. As a result, Decision B spending plan saves $660 a month; a reduction in expenses was required to accomplish the monthly saving target:

1. You upgraded from a single-bedroom apartment to a two-bedroom apartment in order to split the rent with a roommate. Your rent changed from $1,400 to $900.
2. You canceled your cable and started a Netflix account; thus, reducing the expense by $142.
3. You shopped around for car insurance; therefore, you saved $50 by switching car insurance provider.

In Decision C spending plan, you obtained a new job with a pay increase thus increasing your monthly savings to $830, while keeping expenses unchanged.

Tip: *Think of your monthly savings as your monopoly piece making a round trip passing "Go" in Monopoly. Instead of collecting $200 for passing "Go", you collect your monthly savings amount.*

Reviewing, reducing, and eliminating your expenses isn't sufficient enough. You also must track your monthly expenses and desired spending, so you have a full understanding of where each dollar is spent. There are available tools to track your spending in a bank mobile app as well as other mobile apps. If the apps are too much, you can track your spending in a small notebook on a weekly basis. As you get the hang of the process, you can predict your monthly expenses and money available to spend. The final step in the process is planning your spending a few months in advance based on your upcoming obligations and activities, such as a Mother's Day gift, vacation trip, summer concert, etc. That way, you won't take money from your savings account or your monthly savings amount to afford your obligations and activities.

A checking account with a bank is where your expenses and spending are paid from. Your paycheck usually is the source of money in your checking account. When you're ready to set aside money dedicated to monthly savings, you'll transfer the money from your checking account to your savings account. Think of this action as a one-way trip given that money goes into the savings account and should rarely come out. Those rare occasions are for emergencies only. The degree of an emergency varies. I'll say the emergency must be dire, such as a required repair to your car for you to drive back and forth to work.

Tip: *Financial resources recommend your savings account has at least six months of expenses. Desired spending is excluded. For example, Exhibit 3.1 Decision A total expenses are $2,260 for the month; thus, six months of expenses is $13,560.*

Quick Exercise 3.1

Determine six months of expenses for Decision B from Exhibit 3.1

Let Your Money Work for You

While your money sits in a savings account, the money earns interest. Interest is the money a bank pays its savings account owner when money stays in the account for a period of time. As of 2023, big banks are providing 0.01% interest on money in a savings account, less than 1%. This rate is pathetic when compared to the bank earning 500 times that on your savings account balance by lending your money at a 5% interest rate or higher to a borrower. Better yet, the bank can earn 500 times interest on your savings account balance with no risk by holding your money in U.S. Treasury bills, since U.S. Treasury bill rates are at 5% in 2023.

Tip: *U.S. Treasury bills are risk-free investment assets given that the U.S. government has never defaulted on paying the interest and principal back.*

	Rate	Saving Balance Before Interest	Savings Balance After Interest
Bank Interest 1-Month	.01%	$5,000	$5,000.50
U.S. Treasury Bill Interest 1-Month	.43%	$5,000	$5,023.00

Exhibit 3.2 has a comparison between 1-month bank interest vs. 1-month U.S. Treasury bill interest

With an interest rate of less than 1%, your money is a crampy worker in the savings account. You can change this by purchasing the same U.S. Treasury bills that the bank can purchase. U.S. citizens have 900 billion in savings as of 2023.[8] The banks are collecting at least $3.87 billion (.43%) of interest from that money while the people, who worked hard for that money, are receiving $90 million (.01%) of interest. The opportunity for people to earn higher interest is there, but individuals don't capitalize on the opportunity. I suspect the following reasons:

1. A lack of knowledge; being unaware of the higher interest opportunity.
2. The thought of their money being unavailable for emergencies.
3. The thought of losing the money.

The lack of knowledge is due to the flaws of the U.S. education system. The thought of savings being unavailable for emergencies is valid; however, the resolution is quite simple. Don't place all your savings into U.S. Treasury bills. Instead, leave a portion of the money in savings and put the rest in U.S. Treasury bills. For example, leave 50% of your money in a savings account and put the other 50% of your money in U.S. Treasury bills. As an additional precaution, you can purchase U.S. Treasury bills in short-dated maturity periods such as 4, 13, and 26-week bills.

If the goal is to optimize your savings while still having money available for emergencies, then apply the T-Bill Ladder Strategy. Let's say you have $2,000 in your savings account. Place $500 in a 4-week bill, $500 in a 13-week bill, $500 in a 26-week bill, and $500 in a 52-week bill. As a result, you are receiving interest and principal back in different time increments. Your money becomes available as time passes. The last reason, the thought of losing the money, isn't valid. The U.S. government has always paid its debt on time, debt as in U.S. Treasury bills and bonds. Countries and corporations purchase U.S. Treasuries when they want to place their cash in a safe haven, while still receiving interest. As of 2023, China owns $869 billion of U.S. treasuries.[9]

How to Purchase a Treasury Bill

Go to treasurydirect.gov to open an account to purchase treasury bills and bonds. As part of the new account process, you have to link your savings or checking account to the Treasury Direct account. Treasury Direct uses the savings or checking account to withdraw the purchase amount of the treasury bill as well as to return the purchase amount and interest of the treasury bill. Completing the new account process takes a few minutes.

After you have logged in to your account, navigate to the BuyDirect page, which has the treasury options available. Exhibit 3.3 is a snapshot of the BuyDirect page. Exhibit 3.3 TreasuryDirect Buy Page. Since your savings are needed for emergencies at any given time, you do not want to tie up the money for an extended period; therefore, the Bills option in Exhibit 3.3 is the right choice. When you select the Bills option and move to the next webpage, a table is displayed of available bills, their auction dates, and issue dates. See Exhibit 3.4. The bills are by terms (maturities) of 4-week, 8-week, 13-week, 17-week, 26-week and 52-week.

Product Term	Auction Date	Issue Date
4-Week	08-24-2023	08-29-2023
4-Week	08-31-2023	09-05-2023
4-Week	09-07-2023	09-12-2023
4-Week	09-14-2023	09-19-2023

Exhibit 3.4 Available Bills

Exhibit 3.3 TreasuryDirect Buy Page

⭘ 8-Week	10-05-2023	10-10-2023
⭘ 8-Week	10-12-2023	10-17-2023
⭘ 13-Week	08-21-2023	08-24-2023
⭘ 13-Week	08-28-2023	08-31-2023
⭘ 13-Week	10-16-2023	10-19-2023
⭘ 17-WEEK	08-23-2023	08-29-2023

Exhibit 3.4 Available Bills

Notice, in Exhibit 3.4, the interest rate for each bill isn't displayed given that the auction date for each bill hasn't occurred. To have an idea of the bills' possible interest rate after the auction, you can check out the most recently completed auction results by clicking on the View Recent Auction Results link within the webpage. The link is displayed at the end of the available bills table. See Exhibit 3.5.

View recent auction results.

Purchase Amount: $

Source of funds: Bank of America - *****

? Learn more about C of I.

? Learn more about Purchase Limitations.

Schedule Reinvestment

○ Yes   **How many times**   Bills may be scheduled for
                                            reinvestment for up to 2
                                            years.

◉ No

? Learn more about Reinvesting Maturing Proceeds.

Payment Destination

Select a destination for the last maturity payment:

Maturity Payment Destination: Bank of America - *****

Submit **Cancel**

Exhibit 3.5

Here is a quick snapshot of the most recently completed auction results Exhibit 3.6. Based on the prior auction results, you can expect the bill interest rate to be five percent at least. It is important for you to understand that the interest rate displayed in the auction results is annualized. You'll receive 1/4 of the interest rate for the 13-week bill. For the 26-week bill, you'll receive ½ of the interest rate. The bill rates are displayed on an annualized basis, so you can have a direct comparison across each bill interest rate.

Bills	CMBs	Notes	Bonds	TIPS	FRNs

Security Term	CUSIP	Issue Date	Maturity Date	High Rate	Investment Rate
4-Week	912797GT8	08/22/2023	09/19/2023	5.280%	5.390%
8-Week	912797HB6	08/22/2023	10/17/2023	5.280%	5.412%
17-Week	912797HV2	08/22/2023	12/19/2023	5.305%	5.490%
13-Week	912797FK8	08/17/2023	11/16/2023	5.295%	5.456%
26-Week	912797GN1	08/17/2023	02/15/2024	5.290%	5.526%
4-Week	912797GS0	08/15/2023	09/12/2023	5.280%	5.390%
8-Week	912797HA8	08/15/2023	10/10/2023	5.280%	5.412%
17-Week	912797HU4	08/15/2023	12/12/2023	5.310%	5.495%
52-Week	912797GK7	08/10/2023	08/08/2024	5.060%	5.351%

Exhibit 3.6 Auction Results

For example, the 13-week bill with an issue date of 8/17/2023 has a high rate of 5.295% in Exhibit 3.6. The actual rate is 1.33%, which is determined by the following formula to de-annualize the rate. Check out the actual rate conversion table for the other bills in Exhibit 3.7.

Bill	Annualized Rate	Actual Rate	Conversion Method
4-week	5.00%	0.43%	Rate ÷ 365 x 28
8-week	5.00%	0.77%	Rate ÷ 365 x 56
13-week	5.00%	1.25%	Rate ÷ 365 x 91
17-week	5.00%	1.64%	Rate ÷ 365 x 119
26-week	5.00%	2.50%	Rate ÷ 365 x 182
52-week	5.00%	4.99%	Rate ÷ 365 x 364

Exhibit 3.7 Actual Rate Conversion Table

De-Annualize the Rate Formula: Interest Rate ÷ 365 (Number of Days in Year) x 91 (Days in Week x Number of Weeks of the bill

Quick Exercise 3.2

Calculate the actual rate of a 17-week bill at 6.5%

Once you have determined the bill that you want to purchase, select the bill e.g. from the available bills table Exhibit 3.4. You then must enter the dollar amount you want to purchase in the Purchase Amount field. Your savings or checking account number is displayed already in the Source of Funds field. Next, you must determine whether you want to automatically repurchase the bill with the bill principal and interest after the bill matures. If so, select the "Yes" button and enter the number of times you want to automatically repurchase the bill using the Schedule Reinvestment section.

Tip: *The interest rate at the time of the automatic reinvestment purchase differs from the original bill. The change in interest rate is driven by the Federal Reserve action of increasing or decreasing the Fed fund rate. If the federal fund rate does not change between the periods, market volatility can change the interest rate.*

If you don't want to reinvest the principal and interest, select "No". Before clicking the submit button, ensure your savings or checking account number is displayed in the Maturity Payment Destination field. Exhibit 3.8 is the result of completing the preceding actions.

● 26-Week	10-02-2023	10-05-2023
○ 26-Week	10-10-2023	10-12-2023
○ 26-Week	10-16-2023	10-19-2023
○ 52-Week	09-05-2023	09-07-2023
○ 52-Week	10-03-2023	10-05-2023

View recent auction results.

Purchase Amount: $ [1000]

Source of funds: [Bank of America - ***** ⌄]

⑦ Learn more about C of I.

⑦ Learn more about Purchase Limitations.

Schedule Reinvestment

● **Yes**   **How many times** [1]   Bills may be scheduled for reinvestment for up to 2 years.

○ **No**

⑦ Learn more about Reinvesting Maturing Proceeds.

Payment Destination

Select a destination for the last maturity payment:

Maturity Payment Destination: [Bank of America - ***** ⌄]

[Submit] [Cancel]

Exhibit 3.8 Select and Enter Bill Purchase Details

To complete the purchase, click on the submit button, then agree to the purchase on the next webpage. On the issue date, e.g. 10/5/2023, Treasury Direct withdraws the net purchase amount, purchase amount minus interest, from your linked savings or checking account. Let's assume the interest rate on a 26-week bill is 5.2% with a purchase amount of $1,000. The interest is $26; therefore, the net purchase amount withdrawn is $974 ($1,000 - $26).

Quick Exercise 3.3

You purchased a 13-week bill with an interest rate of 5.5%. Your purchase amount is $750. Calculate the net purchase amount that is withdrawn from your savings or checking account.

On the bill's expiration date, Treasury Direct deposits your bill's purchase amount into your linked savings or checking account. In the previous example where your net purchase amount is $974, Treasury Direct deposits $1,000, resulting in a gain of $26.

Other Interest Options

U.S. Treasuries are not the only option available to receive risk-free interest. The other option is a Certificate of Deposit (CD), which pays interest for a certain period. Banks, credit unions, brokerage firms, and special entities such as Sallie Mae offer CDs. U.S. banks and Sallie Mae receive a special nod from me since their CDs are guaranteed by U.S. government FDIC program. The FDIC program guarantees that you'll receive your money and interest no matter what. Depending on the U.S. economy and interest rates, CDs can offer higher interest rates than U.S. Treasuries.

Tip: *The FDIC program guarantee limit amount is $250,000. If you want FDIC guarantee protection for an amount exceeding $250,000, then open an additional CD with another bank or Sallie Mae.*

How to Purchase a CD with Sallie Mae

Go to www.salliemae.com/banking/certificates-of-deposit/ to open an account to a purchase CD. After you have logged in to your account, click on Start a New Application to begin. The following product classes are displayed on the next screen: Money Market Account, savings account, and CDs. Exhibit 3.9 has some of the CDs available for purchase.

sallie mae   CONTACT US   877-346-2756

Certificates of Deposit

Regular Certificates

Select	Products	Minimum Balance for APY	APY	
	6 Month Certificate of Deposit	$2,500	4.80%	Details
	9 Month Certificate of Deposit	$2,500	4.85%	Details
	11 Month Certificate of Deposit	$2,500	4.90%	Details
	12 Month Certificate of Deposit	$2,500	4.95%	Details

Exhibit 3.9 Available CDs by Maturity

Unlike Treasury bills where the purchase amount is at your discretion, Sallie Mae CDs have minimum required purchase amounts of $2,500; see Exhibit 3.9. Once you have selected the CD type, e.g. 6 Month Certificate of Deposit, you are asked whether you want to add a co-owner to the CD. You also are asked whether you want to add a death beneficiary to CD.

Tip: *Death beneficiary allows someone else to receive the CD principal and interest if you are deceased at the CD mature date.*

Next, you have to link your savings or checking account to the Sallie Mae account, so the purchase amount is deducted from the savings or checking account. Lastly, you must review and submit the purchase of the CD. The purchase amount is deducted from your savings or checking account the next day.

Tip: *Unlike Treasury bill purchase, the entire purchase amount is deducted from your savings or checking account.*

When the CD matures, the purchase amount and interest are not deposited into your savings or checking account like a treasury bill. Instead, the purchase amount and interest stay within your Sallie Mae account. As a result, you have the option to reinvest the purchase amount and interest into another CD or transfer the funds to your savings or checking account.

Tip: *Treasury bills have one advantage over CDs; the interest received from treasury bills is exempted from state and local taxes.*

Setting Yourself Part

At this point in time, you understand how to establish your monthly spending plan that includes savings, expenses, and desired spending. You now have the power to transform your financial situation drastically by curbing your desired spending. The money not spent is available to invest into investment securities via a ROTH IRA or personal brokerage. This decision allows you to take more control of your life and puts you ten steps ahead toward being financially independent. There is a significant difference between a ROTH IRA and personal brokerage. A ROTH IRA is another option when investing your money for retirement. You make contributions to a ROTH IRA with money already taxed from your gross pay. One of its advantages is you don't pay taxes on the money withdrawn from the account like an IRA.

Tip: *As your ROTH IRA account balance increases due to contributions, interest, dividends, and capital gains, the balance is exempted from taxation when the money is held in the account for at least five years.*

If you decide to withdraw money from your ROTH IRA account before the age of 59 1/2, you will incur a 10% withdrawal penalty on the amount withdrawn. This 10% withdrawal penalty should sound familiar given that it applies to a 401k and an IRA. Let's say you're seventy years old, retired, and file single. In this particular year, you withdrew $90,000 from your ROTH IRA for living and traveling expenses. Before your retirement, your income was $45,000 per year. Check out the results:

	Working	**Retirement ROTH IRA**
Annual Income	$45,000	$90,000
Income Tax Rate	**22%**	**None**

Exhibit 3.10 Working vs Retirement ROTH IRA Tax Rate

Since your working income was modest, the federal income tax rate was 22%. We won't consider the state income tax rate given it varies by state. As you continued to contribute to your ROTH IRA over time, you accumulated enough money to withdraw $90,000 during your retirement. Given that you chose to use a ROTH IRA account, you avoided federal income taxes on the $90,000 withdrawn.

Quick Exercise 3.4

Your money within a ROTH IRA is exempted from taxation when the money is held in the account for at least five years.

a. True
b. False

Unlike a 401k, IRA and ROTH IRA, a personal brokerage account must pay taxes on dividends, interest income, and realized capital gains. You can open a personal brokerage account with any brokerage provider just as you would with an IRA or a ROTH IRA.

Tip: *Realized capital gains occur when you purchase an investment security such as a stock, then later sell the investment security (stock) for a profit. The difference between the purchase amount and the sold amount is the profit that requires taxation. As of 2023, here are the capital gain tax brackets:*

Your Taxable Income for the Year	Capital Gains Tax
Less than $44,625	0%
Between $44,626 and $492,300	15%
More than $492,300	20%

Exhibit 3.11 Capital Gain Tax Rate by Income Level

In contrast to a 401k, IRA, and ROTH IRA, money can be withdrawn from your personal brokerage account anytime without penalty. There are also no limitations to trading strategies with a personal brokerage account.

Quick Exercise Answers

3.1. $11,568

Multiple monthly expenses amount $1,928 by 6

3.2. 2.12%

.065 (Interest Rate) ÷ 365 (Days in Year) x 119 (13 weeks x 7 Days)

3.3. $736.50

$750 (Purchase Amount) – 13.5 (Interest)

3.4 A (True)

Chapter Test

1. Most financial resources recommend which percentage of monthly income for your savings:
    a. 30%
    b. 15%
    c. 10%
    d. 20%
2. If your monthly expenses are $1,800, how much is needed to have six months of emergency expenses?
3. Which investment option is risk-free?
    a. Stocks
    b. Business Venture
    c. Bitcoin
    d. U.S. Treasury bills and bonds
4. Calculate the actual rate of 26-week bill at 4.8%.
5. A 26-week treasury bill matures in which period:
    a. 3 months
    b. 1 month
    c. 6 months
    d. 1 year
6. What is the strategy to place your savings money in different treasury bills no greater than 52 weeks:
    a. Minimum strategy
    b. Pay Your First Strategy
    c. T-Bill Strategy
    d. High-Risk Strategy

7. CDs cannot be purchased from which entity below:
    a. Banks and Credit Unions
    b. Sallie Mae
    c. Brokerage Provider
    d. Local Government
8. Your CD is guaranteed when purchased from a bank or Sallie Mae.
    a. True
    b. False
9. A personal brokerage account requires you to pay taxes on interest, dividends, and realized capital gains regardless of whether the money is withdrawn from the account or not.
    a. True
    b. False
10. Which retirement account balance is tax exempted when withdrawing money from the account after the money has been held in the account for five years?
    a. 401k
    b. IRA
    c. ROTH IRA

Chapter Test Answers:

1. D (20%)
2. $10,800
3. D (U.S. Treasury bills and bonds)
4. 2.40%

    .480 (Interest Rate) ÷ 360 (Number of Days in Year) x 182 (26 weeks x 7 Days)

5. C (6 months)
6. C (T-Bill Ladder Strategy)
7. D (Local Government)
8. A (True)
9. A (True)
10. C (ROTH IRA)

Chapter 4

Two Traits to Shape Your Financial Mentality

Every year the National Football League (NFL) has a rookie symposium where first-year players get acclimated to professional football. The rookie symposium is a big deal given that 80% of NFL players go broke in their first three years out of the league.[10] In 2011, former NFL player and coach Herm Edwards gave advice at the rookie symposium to players about managing their money: "In life, all you need is one of everything: one car, one house, one piece of jewelry, and one significant other, just one." This principle makes sense whether your occupation results in hundreds, thousands, or millions of dollars. I got to thinking why this advice isn't shared with people who aren't about to make millions of dollars. Despite a single individual income, two cars can't be driven at the same time; furthermore, both cars lose value each day as time passes. While one car is driven, the other one is parked losing value. Better yet, the money used to purchase the second car could have been invested instead. Regardless of the amount of money you earn, the money does you no good if you don't have the right financial mindset.

Financial Discipline

The right financial mindset starts with financial discipline. Without financial discipline, you can forget about sticking to your spending plan or accomplishing your financial goals. Financial discipline entails staying committed to your spending plan and financial goals despite adversities and desires. For example, your close friends want you to go to Cabo, Mexico for a weekend in the spring. Lying beachside soaking up the sun and the amazing water sounds incredible, but if your spending plan can't accommodate the unplanned trip then you must decline the invitation. While saying no to close friends suck, no financial goal is accomplished without sacrifice.

Financial discipline also means doing what it takes to achieve your goal. For instance, you didn't receive a promotion that came with a pay increase. You were planning to place the additional income from the promotion in your personal brokerage to invest. Doing what it takes, you decide to take on a part-time job to supplement the missed promotion income, so you can still invest the additional income. There are three keys to financial discipline:

1. Commitment
2. Do What It Takes
3. Self-Evaluation

No one knows if you are financially disciplined but you. You must hold yourself accountable. When your commitment wavers, don't make excuses. Self-evaluate the root cause of your deterrence, then take the appropriate actions to reaffirm your commitment. An appropriate action is to loosen your stringent monthly savings, so you have a little bit more spending money to enjoy life; thus, you eliminate the impulsive purchases that you have been making lately. If having only one of something doesn't resonate with you, here is another principle you can abide by: if you can't buy an item twice, then don't buy the item at all, whether it is a $100 watch, $500 Gucci bag or $1,000 Mac computer. Living by this code ensures you don't burden yourself with buying something you can barely afford at the time.

Delayed Gratification

The second half of having the right financial mindset is delayed gratification. Let's say, you want to purchase a motorcycle. Delay the purchase of the motorcycle for a year. Place the money you would use to purchase the motorcycle in a 52-week treasury bill. Once the treasury bill matures, a year has passed, and if you still have the desire to purchase the motorcycle, then proceed with the purchase. If not, then you saved yourself thousands of dollars given that you truly didn't want the motorcycle. The motorcycle was fulfilling a temporary desire (impulsive) that no longer exists. You also gained interest from the treasury bill, so your money increased in value while you waited.

Tip: *Wait an extended time before purchasing an item to test your desire for the item.*

Another perk of delayed gratification—it defines your values in life. Those values are reinforced every time you exercise delayed gratification. Given the technology we have at our fingertips along with marketing algorithms, the ability to spend impulsively and compulsively is at its highest; this is one of the reasons why 70% of the U.S. economy is consumption of goods and services. In the long run, you can be a prisoner of the system, manipulated by marketing tactics and others' consumption or you can control your own spending choices and obtain financial independence through your financial goals.

Chapter Test

1. What are three keys for financial discipline?
    a. Hard work, teamwork, ambition
    b. Honesty, courage, respect
    c. Commitment, Do What It Takes, self-evaluation
    d. Determination, skill, luck

2. If you can't buy the item twice, then you...
    a. Should wait three months to buy the item
    b. Should buy it on your credit card
    c. Should borrow money to buy the item
    d. Don't buy the item at all

3. Delayed gratification means waiting an extended period of time before purchasing an item to test your desire for the item.
    a. True
    b. False

4. What is another benefit of practicing delayed gratification?
    a. Makes you impulsive to spend
    b. Define and reinforce your values
    c. Allows a lot of spending in a short time
    d. Encourage spending right away

5. Herm Edwards's advice to NFL players, "In life, all you need is one of everything: one car, one house, one piece of jewelry, and one significant other, just one."
    a. True
    b. False

Chapter Test Answers:

1. C (Commitment, Do What It Takes, Self-Evaluation)

2. D (Don't buy the item at all)

3. A (True)

4. B (Define and reinforce your values

5. A (True)

Chapter 5

Distinguishing Assets from Liabilities

The relationship between assets and liabilities is equivalent to gardens and weeds. With tender care and attention, a garden will flourish. The garden flourishes enough to where minimum attention is required. As you're sleeping and working, the garden does the hard work of producing vegetables and fruits. The same goes for assets as they grow in value and produce income (money) over time.

Weeds are a detriment to your garden. If not proactively managed, weeds stifle the growth of your vegetables and fruits. In the end, weeds erode your garden's potential. The garden's contagion then spreads to your surrounding grass. Liabilities (debts) have the same effect on your assets and income. Liabilities sack you with a burden that reduces your net worth and financial freedom.

Tip: *Assets minus liabilities equals net worth.*

Types of Assets

Before we get into the effects of liabilities, let's cover the various types of assets as well as their primary purpose. An asset has the ability to decrease and increase in value over time. There are some assets that can produce income. Exhibit 5.1 is an illustration of the asset types along with their primary purpose: value appreciation, income, or both.

Type	Value Appreciation	Income	Both
A Business			x
Art Paintings	x		
Cash			
Commodities (Oil, Silver, Gold, Copper)	x		
Corporate Bonds		x	
CDs		x	
Money Markets		x	
Municipal bonds		x	
Exchange Traded Funds			x
Intellectual Property			x
Mutual Funds			x
Real Estate			x
Stocks			x
Treasury bills and bonds		x	

Exhibit 5.1 Asset Types

Per the illustration, the income assets are the debt nature assets, while the value appreciation assets increase in value over time. Then, there are a few assets that give you both purposes. There is a misconception that cars, jewelry, and furniture are assets since they hold value; however, their value decreases over time. When an item's value only decreases over time, the item isn't an asset. In addition to depreciating in value, cars, jewelry, and furniture also have maintenance and insurance requirements that cost money.

Tip: *Debt nature asset—you lend your money to a borrower (government, corporation, bank) for a set period. The borrower pays back the loaned money plus the promised interest.*

Tip: *When an item loses value over time, it is called depreciation.*

In Exhibit 5.1, cash is listed as an asset but does not generate income or increase in value. When you consider inflation, it decreases the value of cash over time. Think of cash as a temporary asset since cash is held temporarily to pay expenses, debt obligations as well as to purchase assets. Determining the amount of cash you want to have available is tricky. Too much cash available and you're undermining its ability to generate income and to purchase assets for appreciation. Too little cash available and you risk your ability to pay unexpected expenses or emergencies. The same decision dilemma occurs when playing Monopoly:

Decision A–Purchase the property thus leaving you low on cash. You take the risk of making a trip around the board to collect $200 while trying not to land on other players' property.

Decision B–You skip the property purchase since luck hasn't been in your favor when comes to landing on other players' properties. As a result, you have plenty of cash available to pay unexpected rent.

Decision C–You purchase the property that does not compromise your cash available; therefore, you have enough cash to pay unexpected rent and taxes.

Performance of an Asset

All assets aren't created equal. Certain assets outperform others. Some assets come with a higher level of risk. To highlight these two points, Exhibit 5.2 has the value appreciation for a few asset types from 2018 to 2022. Each asset purchase amount is $1,000 in 2018.

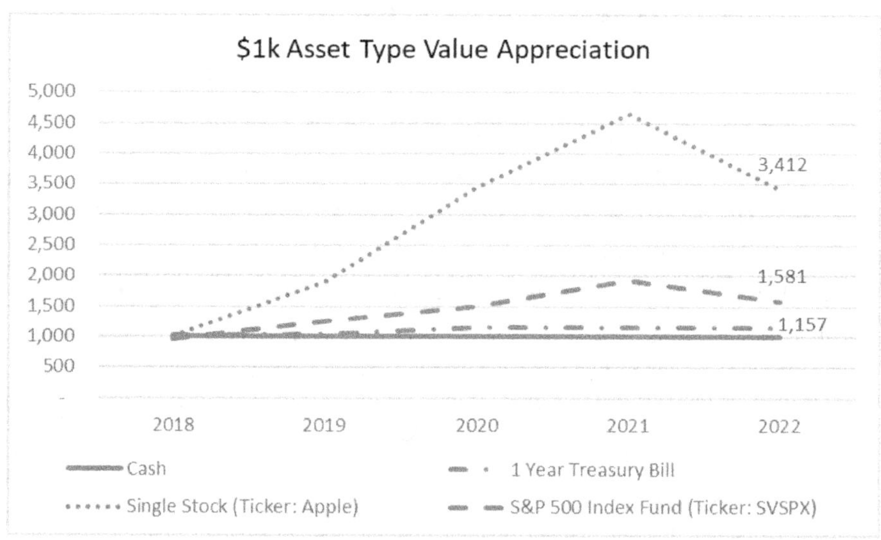

Exhibit 5.2 Value Appreciation for a Few Assets

The biggest performer of the period is the single stock. Investing in a single stock is high risk, high reward. This particular stock, APPL (Apple), resulted in the asset appreciating three-fold. Runner up to the single stock performance is the S&P 500 Index Fund. The fund intends to mimic the S&P 500 index, which is a U.S. board market portfolio with 500 individual stocks. By purchasing the S&P 500 index fund, single-stock investment risk is eliminated. Since the fund is invested in 500 stocks, on any given trading day, some stocks' prices decline, while other prices rise. The sum of the stocks' declines (losses) and rises (gains) offset in either direction. That action doesn't occur with a single stock. You reap all the losses or the gains when invested in a single stock.

Tip: *Investing in more than one stock, fund index, or asset type, is called diversification. Diversification reduces huge losses (risks) but limits maximum gains (rewards).*

The risk-free investment one-year treasury bill yields a small margin of value appreciation due to the interest income received each year. The $1,000 in cash is unchanged throughout the period. In actuality, the $1,000 in cash at the end of the period can't buy the same goods or services that the $1,000 could buy at the beginning of the period due to inflation, so the cash loses value.

Liabilities

When you don't have enough cash for a large purchase or you elect not to spend all your cash for a large purchase, you must take on a liability to purchase the item. Common liabilities are car notes, credit card balances, line of credit, student loans, personal loans, medical bills, mortgages, and home equity loans. Except for medical bills, each liability comes with paying interest along with the amount borrowed for the purchase. Liabilities become a problem when:

1. Liability payments are a substantial amount of your income.
2. Your income is reduced unexpectedly.
3. Liability payments expand across multiple years thus layering on top of future financial obligations.

Tip: *A good debt-to-income ratio is 36% or lower, since it is lenders' preferred percentage.*

Debt to Income Ratio = Each Monthly Liability Payment Sumed ÷ Monthly Income

Exercise 5.1

Your monthly liability payments consist of $50 credit card, $230 car note, $145 student loan, and $1,200 mortgage. Your monthly income is $3,000. Calculate your debt-to-income ratio.

When your liabilities are out of control, they have the following effects on your financials:

1. Selling an asset to pay off a liability.
2. Inability to take advantage of future asset opportunities.
3. Requires additional payments to pay off the li-ability sooner thus tying up more income.
4. Destroy your morale, e.g. causes stress.

Think long and hard before you commit to liability by asking yourself the following questions:

1. Will I still enjoy this item thirty days, six months, and three years from now?
2. What does my debt-to-income ratio increase to with this new liability?
3. What if my income decreases by 20%, do I still have enough income to afford the liability payment along with my other expenses and savings?

You may enjoy the item that the liability brought in the moment. But when the enjoyment wears off, the liability payment remains. Keep this in mind when you're deciding to finance a purchase.

Quick Exercise Answers

1. 54%

   $1,625 (Sum of the liability payments) ÷ $3,000 (Income) = .54 or 54%

Chapter Test

1. Select an asset that appreciates in value:
   a. Treasury Bill
   b. Car
   c. Cash
   d. Art Painting
2. Debt nature assets, the borrower pays back the lent money plus the promised interest.
   a. True
   b. False
3. Cash is considered a liability.
   a. True
   b. False
4. If Thomas has $50,000 in liabilities, $10,000 in cash and $100,000 in stocks, what is Thomas net worth:
   a. $50,000
   b. $10,000
   c. $60,000
   d. $70,000
5. Select an answer that has value appreciation and income:
   a. Real Estate, Stocks and Exchange Traded Funds
   b. Car, Jewelry and Furniture
   c. Cash, CD, and Corporate Bonds
   d. Art Painting
6. What is the purpose of diversification:
   a. To maximum gains (wins)
   b. To reduce risk (losses)
   c. To eliminate all risk
   d. To invest

7. Sarah has the following liability payments every month: $150 car note, $50 credit card payment, $500 student loan. Her income every month is $2,000. What is Sarah's debt-to-income ratio?
    a. 40%
    b. 25%
    c. 35%
    d. 15%

8. Lenders (banks) prefer potential borrowers to have a debt-to-income ratio of 36% or less
    a. True
    b. False

9. When an item loses value over time, it is called:
    a. Appreciation
    b. Depreciation
    c. Risk
    d. Liability

10. What is one of the effects when your liabilities become unmanageable:
    a. Your assets rise
    b. Result in you selling an an asset to pay off a liability.
    c. You have more income to spend
    d. You can purchase more assets
    e. You receive more interest from your assets

Chapter Test Answers

1. D (Art Painting)

2. A (True)

3. B (False)

4. C ($60,000)

   $100,000 (sum of assets) minus $50,000 (sum of liabilities) = $60,000 (net worth)

5. A (Real Estate, Stocks, and Exchange Traded Funds)

6. C (To reduce risks (losses))

7. C (35%)

   700 (sum of liability payments) ÷ $2,000 income = .35

8. A (True)

9. B (Depreciation)

10. B (Result in you selling an asset to pay off a liability.)

Chapter 6

How to Calculate a Loan Monthly Payment

Your first major liability as a young adult is purchasing a new or used car. This moment comes with a lot of excitement and anxiety. The excitement of driving a car that you want instead of your parent's old car. The anxiety of going through the car buying process for the first time. Couple that with borrowing a large amount of money, and the feeling is overwhelming. Knowing the liability effect on your debt-to-income ratio when deciding to borrow money isn't good enough. Understanding the liability monthly payment affects whether the cost of the liability works for you. The cost of a liability is driven by the borrowing amount (purchase amount), the interest rate, and the time to pay back the liability.

Determine a Loan Monthly Payment

To determine the borrowing amount of a loan that you can afford, you must have an idea of the borrowing amount monthly payment. There are a few resources at your disposal to calculate the loan monthly payment. The first is a physical hand-held financial calculator such as Texas Instruments BA II Plus. The second is a financial calculator app that is downloadable on your cell phone such as Financial Calculators by Bishinews. Any other financial calculator app works as well. The third is a financial calculator on a bank (lender) website. Through the chapter exercises, the usage of the financial calculator app is referenced. Exhibit 6.1 is a preview of the financial calculator app opened.

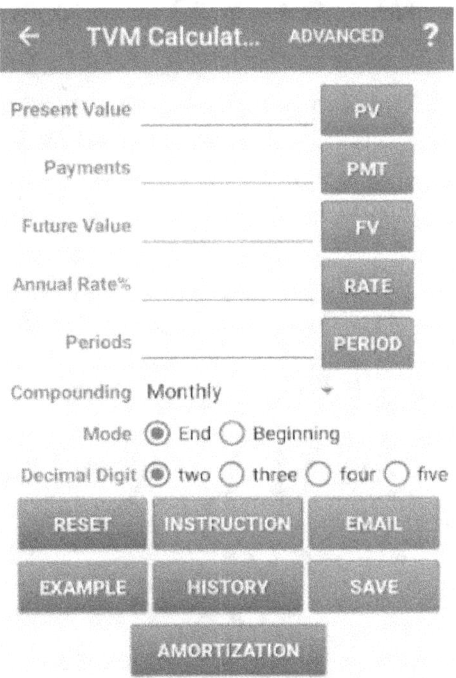

Exhibit 6.1 Preview of Financial Calculator

To generate the loan monthly payment within the calculator, you must enter values in the Present Value, Annual Rate %, and Periods fields. Then, click on the PMT button for the monthly payment to display. Malcolm was in the market for his own car two years out of college. His parent's old Buick finally gave out on him. Malcolm knew the car was on its last leg figuratively, so he started searching for cars in the area using cars.com, autotrader.com, and local dealerships' websites. A few cars interested him, but he was set on the 2011 Chevrolet Malibu. He noticed the car's purchase price was $17,000. The estimated interest rate to borrow money for the car was 5%. He preferred to pay off the loan (liability) in four years. Exhibit 6.2 has the calculator monthly payment of a $17,000 loan based on the conditions mentioned.

Exhibit 6.2 Results of $17,000 Loan Monthly Payment

The loan monthly payment is $391.50. Since the compounding field is set to monthly, the monthly equivalent of four years is entered in the period field. While the monthly payment amount didn't scare off Malcolm, he became curious about the monthly payment, if he borrowed the money on a three or five-year payback period. Exhibit 6.3 has a comparison of loan monthly payments for the payback periods.

	3 Yr	4 Yr	5 Yr
Present Value	17,000.00	17,000.00	17,000.00
Payments	509.51	391.50	320.81
Future Value			
Annual Rate%	5	5	5
Periods	36	48	60
Compounding	Monthly	Monthly	Monthly
Total Cost of the Loan	18,342.36	18,792.00	19,248.60
Interest Cost	1,342.36	1,792.00	2,248.60

Exhibit 6.3 Monthly Payments for the Payback Periods

The loan monthly payment significantly increases from the $300 to the $500 range when reducing the loan payback period to three years. While the five-year payback period provides some comfort with a reduction in the loan monthly payment, a common mistake by borrowers is to focus so much on the loan monthly payment that they overlook the total cost to pay back the borrowed money (loan), which is the Total Cost of the Loan. A decision to opt for the five-year payback period comes with the lowest monthly payment but the highest total cost of the loan.

Tip: *The shorter the loan payback period, the less interest you pay when the borrowing amount and interest rate are unchanged.*

Total Cost of the Loan: Monthly Payment Amount x Periods

Interest Cost: Total Cost of the Loan - Purchase Price

Tip: *Extending the payback period on a loan decreases the monthly payment, while reducing the payback period on a loan increases the monthly payment amount.*

Quick Exercise 6.2

What is Exercise 6.2 total cost of the loan and interest cost?

Before Malcolm decided to visit the car dealership that had a blue 2011 Chevrolet Malibu, he was advised by his father to consider the possibility of being offered a lower or higher interest rate than anticipated from the lender or the dealership. Malcolm's father knew the loan interest rate is another way the loan monthly payment is affected. Check out the results of the loan monthly payment when the interest rate changes in Exhibit 6.4.

	4 Yr	4 Yr	4 Yr
Present Value	17,000.00	17,000.00	17,000.00
Payments	376.28	391.50	431.16
Future Value			
Annual Rate%	3	5	10
Periods	48	48	48
Compounding	Monthly	Monthly	Monthly
Total Cost of the Loan	18,061.44	18,792.00	20,695.68
Interest Cost	1,061.44	1,792.00	3,695.68

Exhibit 6.4 Loan Monthly Payment Amounts For Various Interest Rates

The interest rate changes in Exhibit 6.4 caused the loan monthly payment to decrease by $20 for the 3% interest rate or to increase by $40 for the 10% interest rate. Bigger picture, the amount of interest paid over the loan payback period more than doubles when the loan interest rate changes from 5% to 10%. Refer back to the interest cost row in Exhibit 6.4. The total interest for the 3% interest rate loan decreases by 60% compared to the 5% interest rate loan. The last piece of advice Malcolm received came from his mother. She told

Malcolm to consider the possibility that the car's total purchase price could exceed $17,000. Should he assess the loan monthly payment, if he decided to decrease or increase the borrowing amount for the loan? Take a look at Exhibit 6.5 results of the borrowing amount change.

	4 Yr	4 Yr	4 Yr
Present Value	12,000.00	17,000.00	22,000.00
Payments	276.35	391.50	506.64
Future Value			
Annual Rate%	5	5	5
Periods	48	48	48
Compounding	Monthly	Monthly	Monthly
Total Cost of the Loan	13,264.80	18,792.00	24,318.72
Total Interest Cost	1,264.80	1,792.00	2,318.72

Exhibit 6.5 Monthly Payment Amounts For Various Borrowing Amounts

Increasing the original borrowing amount from $17,000 to $22,000 results in the loan monthly payment hitting the $500 range like the three-year payback loan in Exhibit 6.3. The loan monthly payment drops below the $300 range with the borrowing amount at $12,000. When Malcolm walked into the dealership with the blue Chevrolet Malibu, he was equipped with information to make a sound decision.

Determine A Loan Interest Rate Based on the Monthly Payment

When you're sitting at the deal table with the car salesman or saleswoman, they present to you the final borrowing amount, loan payback period, and the monthly payment based on running your credit through their network of lenders. Often, the presentation of the information does not contain the loan interest rate. In this moment, your ability to arrive at the loan interest rate based on the information provided is critical. Car dealerships (their network of lenders) attempt to deal high interest rates to potential customers.

Exhibit 6.6 Results of $21,000 Loan Interest Rate

For instance, the car salesman comes to the deal table with a final borrowing amount of $21,000, five-year payback period, and monthly payment of $521.90. Using the financial calculator to generate the interest rate for the loan, you must enter values in the Present Value, Payments, and Periods fields. Enter the Payment amount with a negative sign in front of the value. If you don't, the calculator computes an error message for the interest rate. Click on the Interest Rate% button for the interest rate to display. Exhibit 6.6 has the interest rate result for the loan. While you could possibly accommodate the monthly payment amount of $521.90, a car loan with an interest rate of 17% is in the higher range of average car interest rates, especially if your credit score is fair or better.

Tip: *Banks display starting interest rates on their auto loans via their websites. Use the banks' starting interest rates as a beginning point to determine a loan monthly payment.*

Quick Exercise 6.3

Determine the interest rate for a loan with a borrowing amount of $30,000, a six-year payback period and a monthly payment of $634.35.

Quick Exercise Answers

1. $386.66

    Enter into a financial calculator: PV $20,000, Interest Rate% 6, Periods 60, then compute Payment.

2. $23,199.60 and $3,199.36

    Total Cost of the Loan: $386.66 (Payment) x 60 (Period Months) = $23,199.60

    Interest Cost: $23,199.60 (Total Cost of the Loan) – Interest Cost ($3,199.36)

3. 15%

    Enter into a financial calculator: PV $30,000, Payment - $634.35, Periods 72, then compute Interest Rate%.

Chapter Test

1. Determine the monthly payment amount of a $32,000 loan with an interest rate of 5% and payback period of six years.
2. You secured a $40,000 loan with an interest rate of 10%, a payback period of four years, and a monthly payment of $1,014.50. What is the total cost of the loan and the interest cost?
3. Determine the interest rate for a loan with a borrowing amount of $8,000, a two-year payback period, and a monthly payment of $372.86.
4. Which one of the debts below is a revolving credit?
   a. Term Loan
   b. Student Loan
   c. Credit Card
   d. Auto Loan

Chapter Test Answers:

1. $515.36

    Enter into a financial calculator: PV $36,000, Interest Rate% 5, Periods 72, then compute Payment.

2. Total Cost of Loan $48,696 and Interest Cost $8,696

    Total Cost of Loan: $1,014.50 (Monthly Payment) x 48 (Payback Period Months) = $48,696

    Interest Cost: $48,696 (Total Cost of Loan) – $40,000 (Loan Amount) = $8,696

3. 11%

    Enter into a financial calculator: PV $8,000, Periods 24, Payment -372.86 then compute Interest Rate%.

    $6,500 (Credit Card Balance) x .145 (Interest Rate) x 0.0849 (31/365) = $80.05

5. C (Credit Card)

Chapter 7

How to Calculate a Credit Card and a Line of Credit Monthly Interest

More times than not, the frequent use of your credit is through your credit card, unless you plan to constantly take loans out for cars and residential properties. A credit card is used for all types of spending, but ideally, the purpose of a credit card is to purchase an item or a service in the moment when you don't have enough money to purchase the item. Before the month ends, you pay off the item purchase amount on the credit card. I said ideally, because it is common for the full purchase amount to go unpaid before the month's end, since the cardholder doesn't have money available via his or her monthly income. As a result, a balance is left on the credit card. Interest is applied to the credit card balance for the month.

Understanding the amount of interest charged (applied) to the credit card balance puts you in a better position to manage the credit card balance and the monthly expense. You're also more likely to put together a successful plan to pay off the credit card balance. If you intend to avoid paying interest on the credit card balance, be mindful that some credit card periods may end on the 25th or 27th of each month instead of the last day of the month. You must have the credit card balance paid off before 25th or 27th, end of the day.

Tip: *You only accumulate interest on a credit card when you don't pay off the credit card balance before the end of the credit card period's month.*

There are three factors required to determine the credit card interest for the month: 1. Credit Card Balance Amount, 2. Interest Rate and 3. Day Count Convention. The first factor, credit card balance, is on your monthly statement or online summary. The interest rate is established when you open the credit card and located in the disclosure documents. The last factor, day count convention, requires some math.

Day Count Convention: Days in the Month ÷ Days in Calendar Year

When determining the days in the month, you must include weekends and holidays. The total days in the calendar year are 365. E.g., a credit card period is August; as a result, the day count convention is .0849.

Day Count Convention: 31 Days (August) ÷ 365 (Days in Calendar Year) = .0849

Use the formula below to determine the interest for the credit card month.

Credit Card Interest: Credit Card Balance x Interest Rate x Day Count Conversion

For example, Ashley spent in August $500 on a shopping spree and $750 on her airplane ticket to Las Vegas for a girl's trip. Her credit card balance is $1,250 at the end of the month. Her interest rate on the credit card is 18%. As a result, the interest is $19.10 for the period.

Credit Card Period Interest: $1,250 x .18 x .0849 = 19.10

Quick Exercise 7.1

For December, your credit card balance is $3,500 with an interest rate of 16.5%. What is the credit card period interest?

Determine a Line of Credit Balance Interest for the Month

A line of credit offers a few advantages over a credit card such as a lower interest rate and a higher credit limit. The cash on the credit limit is available for withdrawal for a line of credit, while a credit card may or may not come with a cash advance limit. If it does, then the credit card has fees associated with the cash advance limit, unlike a line of credit. The stark difference between a line of credit vs. a credit card is that a credit card's interest is determined after the period ends. You go 30 (31) days without interest accumulating on a credit card. For a line of credit, the interest is determined daily on the line of credit balance; therefore, the interest accumulates as soon as the line of credit is used. As a result, you can't avoid paying interest for the period when there is a balance on the line of credit, not even for a single day. The interest accumulation during the period stops on the day you pay off the balance. There are three factors required to determine the daily line of credit interest: Line of Credit Balance, Interest Rate, and Daily Count Convention.

Daily Count Convention: 1 (Day) ÷ 365 (Days in Calendar Year) = .002740

Use the formula below to determine the daily interest for the line of credit.

Daily Line of Credit Interest: Line of Credit Balance x Interest Rate x Daily Count Conversion

For example, on the 5th day of July, you used the line of credit amount of $4,000. You paid off the $4,000 balance four days later, on the 9th day of July. The line of credit balance for the rest of the month remained zero. Your interest rate on the line of credit is 8%. Exhibit 7.1 illustrates the daily interest calculation from the 1st through 9th of July and the total interest accumulated during the period.

Day	Date	Balance	Interest Rate	Daily Day Convention	Daily Interest
1	7/1/2023	$0.00	8%	0.002740	-
2	7/2/2023	$0.00	8%	0.002740	-
3	7/3/2023	$0.00	8%	0.002740	-
4	7/4/2023	$0.00	8%	0.002740	-
5	7/5/2023	$4,000.00	8%	0.002740	0.8767
6	7/6/2023	$4,000.00	8%	0.002740	0.8767
7	7/7/2023	$4,000.00	8%	0.002740	0.8767
8	7/8/2023	$4,000.00	8%	0.002740	0.8767
9	7/9/2023	$0.00	8%	0.002740	-
				Total	3.51

Exhibit 7.1 Daily Interest and Total Interest Accumulated

The daily interest for periods 4th through 8th is $.8767.

Daily Line of Credit Interest: $4,000 x .08 x .0027 = .8767

Add each day's daily interest for the monthly end period to determine the total interest for the period. In this case, the total interest is $3.51, since the line of credit balance didn't change after the 9th day of the monthly period. In the same example, what if the balance did change after the 9th day? Let's say the balance increases to $7,000 on the 9th of July, then the balance is paid on the 15th of July. Exhibit 7.2 displays the change in daily interest from 9th through 15th of July as well as the interest accumulated in the period.

Day	Date	Balance	Interest Rate	Daily Day Convention	Daily Interest
1	7/1/2023	$0.00	8%	0.002740	-
2	7/2/2023	$0.00	8%	0.002740	-
3	7/3/2023	$0.00	8%	0.002740	-
4	7/4/2023	$0.00	8%	0.002740	-
5	7/5/2023	$4,000.00	8%	0.002740	$0.8767
6	7/6/2023	$4,000.00	8%	0.002740	$0.8767
7	7/7/2023	$4,000.00	8%	0.002740	$0.8767
8	7/8/2023	$4,000.00	8%	0.002740	$0.8767
9	7/9/2023	$7,000.00	8%	0.002740	$1.5342
10	7/10/2023	$7,000.00	8%	0.002740	$1.5342
11	7/11/2023	$7,000.00	8%	0.002740	$1.5342
12	7/12/2023	$7,000.00	8%	0.002740	$1.5342
12	7/13/2023	$7,000.00	8%	0.002740	$1.5342
12	7/14/2023	$7,000.00	8%	0.002740	$1.5342
12	7/15/2023	$0.00	8%	0.002740	-
				Total	$14.71

Exhibit 7.2 Change of Daily Interest During the Period

Notice the daily interest increased to $1.5342 from $.8767 due to the increase in the balance to $7,000.

Quick Exercise 7.2

On the 4th day of April, you used the line of credit amount of $2,000. On the 12th of April, you used the line of credit again for $6,000; thus, the balance increased to $8,000. You paid off the $8,000 balance on the 20th of the same month. The line of credit interest rate is 7%. What is the total interest for the April month period?

Quick Exercise Answers

1. $49.05

$3,500 (Credit Card Balance) x .165 (Interest Rate) x 0.0849 (31/365) = $49.05

2. $15.34

Chapter Test

1. What factors are required to calculate the interest on a credit card?
    a. Credit Card Balance, Cash Advance Rate, and Day Count Convention
    b. Credit Card Balance, Interest Rate, and Calendar Month
    c. Credit Card Balance, Interest Rate, and Day Count Convention
    d. Cash Advance Balance, Cash Advance Rate, and Calendar Month
2. You can avoid accumulating interest on your credit card by paying off the credit card balance before the end of the monthly period.
    a. True
    b. False
3. For March, the credit card balance is $6,500 with an interest rate of 14.5%. What is the credit card period interest?
4. For May, your line of credit balance was $0 until you withdrew $2,500 on the 20th and an additional $5,000 on 27th. The balance for the month closed at $7,500. Your interest rate on the line of credit is 9.5%. What is the total interest for the period?

Chapter Test Answers:

1. C (Credit Card Balance, Interest Rate, and Day

2. A (True)

3. $80.05

    $6,500 (Credit Card Balance) x .145 (Interest Rate) x 0.0849 (31/365) = $80.05

4. $14.31

    $2,500 (Line of Credit Balance) x 0.095 (Interest Rate) x 0.0192 (//365) = $4.55

    $7,000 (Line of Credit Balance) x 0.095 (Interest Rate) x 0.0137 (5/365) = $9.76

    $4.55 + $9.76 = $14.31

Chapter 8

Ways to Eliminate Debt: Strategies, Tips, and Resources to Pay Off What You Owe

Once you have access to credit, the ability to run up debt is as easy as turning on a faucet. Inexperienced users of debt are like children at the bathroom faucet—quick to turn the faucet to full blast, leaving a mess of water to clean up. In this chapter, you'll learn ways to clean up the mess of water (debt) starting with the method known as Debt Stacking.

Debt Stacking involves making a budget, listing your debts by size or interest rate, and paying extra money toward the highest priority debt while making minimum payments on the others. You are required to perform the following actions for the debt stacking method to work:

1. Stop creating new debt and increasing the balances on current debts.
2. Rank the debts from highest to lowest based on the debt interest rate.

3. If possible, lower your credit card interest rate by doing balance transfer.
4. Pay the minimum payment amount on all your debts every month.
5. Determine how much of your income you can allocate toward paying your debts every month.

Let's put the debt stacking method into practice. Exhibit 8.1 has your outstanding debts, current balances, interest rates, minimum payments, monthly interest based on current balances, and current monthly payments.

Rank	Debt	Current Balance	Interest Rate	Minimum Payment	Monthly Interest Based on Current Balance*	Current Monthly Payments
1	Credit Card # 1	$10,000	18%	$100	$153	$200
2	Credit Card # 2	$5,000	13%	$50	$55	$150
3	Line of Credit	$3,000	8%	$50	$20	$100
4	Car Loan[1]	$20,000	5%$	$377.42	N/A	$377.42

Exhibit 8.1 Outstanding Debts
The maximum days, 31 days in the month, is used to calculate the monthly interest based on current balance
[1] *Term loan with a payback period 60 months*

The debts are ranked with Credit Card # 1 listed as number 1 given it has the highest interest rate. The rest of the debt ranking is in the Rank column. Let's assume you cannot afford to allocate extra income to your current monthly debt payments; therefore, your total current monthly debt payments remain at $827.42, which is the sum of individual debt current monthly payments in Exhibit 8.1. The key principle in the debt stacking method is to redistribute the current monthly payments by paying the largest payment amount on the highest interest rate debt, while also paying the minimum payment on the revolving credit and the fixed payment on the non-revolving (term) credit.

Tip: *Credit cards and line of credit are revolving credit, while car loans, mortgage, personal loans, student loans are non-revolving (term) credit.*

Exhibit 8.2 illustrates the redistribution of the current monthly payments to future monthly payments.

Rank	Debt	Interest Rate	Current Time to Pay off Balance	Current Monthly Payments	Future Monthly Payments
1	Credit Card # 1	18%	93 months	$200	$340
2	Credit Card # 2	13%	42 months	$150	$60
3	Line of Credit	8%	33 months	$100	$50
4	Car Loan	5%	60 months	$377.42	$377.42
			Total	$827.42	$827.42

Exhibit 8.2

The car loan and line of credit future monthly payments are set to their minimum payment amounts. Credit card # 2 future monthly payment is set $10 over its minimum payment of $50, given that its current monthly interest is greater than the minimum payment amount. If the future monthly payment is not set above the monthly interest, then the credit card balance increases. Remember, the debt balances can't increase in the debt stacking process. The rest of the future monthly payment funds are allocated to credit card # 1's monthly payment of $340. As a result of the future monthly payment for credit card # 1, the estimated time to pay off the credit card balance changes from 93 to 39 months. You can use the financial calculator app to arrive at 39 months by entering the credit card's current balance as the Present Value, the credit card's current interest rate as Annual Rate % and the future monthly payment amount as the PMT. Then, click on the Period button for the period value to display. Exhibit 8.3 has the financial calculator payoff period results.

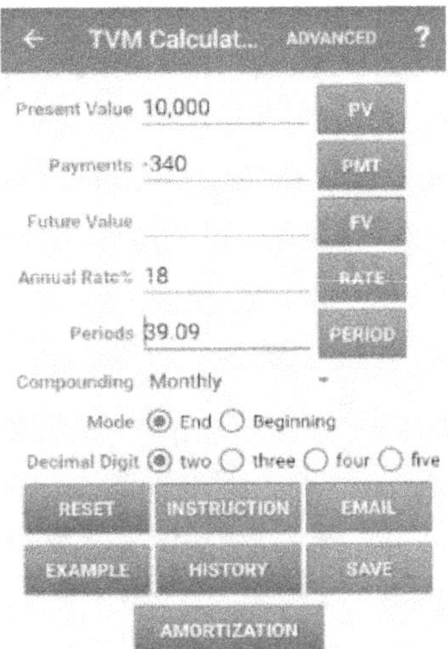

Exhibit 8.3 Results of Credit Card # 1
New Payoff Period

After the 39 months, you then apply the $340 monthly payment funds to credit card # 2's monthly payment. See the new distribution of monthly payments in Exhibit 8.4.

Rank	Debt	Interest Rate	Current Balance	Future Monthly Payments	Future Time to Pay off Balance
1	Credit Card # 2	13%	$4,716	$400	13 months
2	Line of Credit	8%	$1,673	$50	38 months
3	Car Loan	5%	$7,574	$377.42	21 months
			Total	$827.42	

Exhibit 8.4 New Distribution of Monthly Payments After 39 Months

Credit card # 2's monthly payment is now $400, $340 plus the previous monthly payment amount of $60. After 13 months, credit card # 2 is paid off. You then repeat the process again of applying the available funds to the next highest interest rate debt. In this case, the next highest interest rate debt is the line of credit. There is a slight uptick in the future pay off period for the line of credit from the original

33 months in Exhibit 8.2 to 38 months in Exhibit 8.4 since the original pay off period was based on the monthly payment of $100 vs the future monthly payment of $50. The car loan continues its downward course to a zero balance with only 21 months remaining. After 13 months, there are two debts remaining: the line of credit and the car loan with a balance of $1,148 and $2,963 respectively. Exhibit 8.5 displays the distribution of monthly payments after 13 months.

Rank	Debt	Interest Rate	Current Balance	Future Monthly Payments	Future Time to Pay off Balance
1	Line of Credit	8%	$1,148	$450	2.5 months
2	Car Loan	5%	$2,963	$377.42	8 months
			Total	$827.42	

Exhibit 8.5 Distribution of Monthly Payments After 13 Months

Given the future monthly payment for the line of credit is $450, the line of credit balance is paid off in 2.5 months. The car loan has 8 months of payments left. After the 2.5 months have passed and the line of credit is paid off, the car loan is the last debt remaining with 5.5 months until its payoff. Exhibit 8.6 illustrates the car loan pay off period change from 5.5 months to 2.5 months.

Rank	Debt	Interest Rate	Current Balance	Current Monthly Payments	Future monthly Payments
1	Car Loan	5%	$2,048	$377.42	$827.42

Exhibit 8.6 Car Loan Pay Off Period Reduction

Repeating the process of applying the available funds to the next debt, the funds are applied to the car loan monthly payment. As a result, the car loan monthly payment increases by $450 thus, shortening the pay off period to 2.5 months. Thanks to the debt stacking method, the debts were paid off three years earlier than initially planned, saving nearly $3,500 in unnecessary interest. Exhibit 8.7 summarizes the outcomes of the original plan vs. the debt stacking plan.

Debt Payment	Payback Period	Total Interest Paid
Original Plan	7.75 Years	$12,695
Debt Stacking Plan	4.75 Years	$9,163

Exhibit 8.7 Outcome of Original Plan vs. Debt Stacking Plan.

Quick Exercise 8.1

Using the debt stacking method, how many months does it take to pay off all debts below with $800 available for monthly payments?

Rank	Debt	Current Balance	Interest Rate	Minimum Payment	Monthly Interest Based on Current Balance*
1	Credit Card # 1	$12,000	14%	$100	$143
2	Line of Credit	$6,000	6%	$50	$31
3	Student Loan[1]	$35,000	5%	$276.78	N/A

Exhibit 8.8

**The maximum days, 31 days in the month, is used to calculate the monthly interest based on current balance*

1 Term loan with a payback period 180 months

One Extra Payment

The other way to eliminate debt sooner is through the one extra payment method. For instance, Kim bought a house with a 30-year $300,000 mortgage loan at 4% interest rate. Her monthly payment amount is $1,432.24. By applying one extra payment every year to the loan, she can reduce the pay off period to 26 years. If Kim doesn't have $1,432.24 once a year to make the extra payment, she can divide the extra payment amount by 12, which is $119.35. Then, pay the monthly payment of $1,432.24 plus the $119.35 each month throughout the loan period. Doing so results in paying off the loan four years and one month sooner than expected. Exhibit 8.9 displays the results of the original loan outcome vs. the original loan with one extra payment method.

	Original	Original Plus One Extra Payment
Present Value	300,000.00	300,000.00
Payments	$1,432.24	$1,551.59
Future Value		
Annual Rate%	4	4
Periods	360	311
Compounding	Monthly	Monthly
Total Cost of the Loan	$516,606	$484,096
Total Interest Cost	$216,606	$184,096

Exhibit 8.9 Original vs Original Loan One Extra Payment

The difference between the two periods is 49 months, equivalent to 4 years and one month. Kim also saves $32,510 in interest by using the one extra payment method. Let's say she desires to pay off the same 30-year loan in 15 years. The extra payment required monthly is $786.82.

Tip: *The financial calculator app covered earlier in the chapter can determine the payoff period with the extra payment method applied on a monthly basis.*

Finding the extra payment benefit for one extra payment per year is a bit more complex using the financial calculator app. Instead of using this complex approach, you can use a mortgage payoff calculator. There are plenty of mortgage payoff calculators available on the internet. use the mortgage payoff calculator calculator.net/mortgage-payoff-calculator website[11].

From the example earlier, perhaps Kim does have one extra payment of $1,432.24 to pay each year, she visits the calculator.net/mortgage-payoff-calculator website.

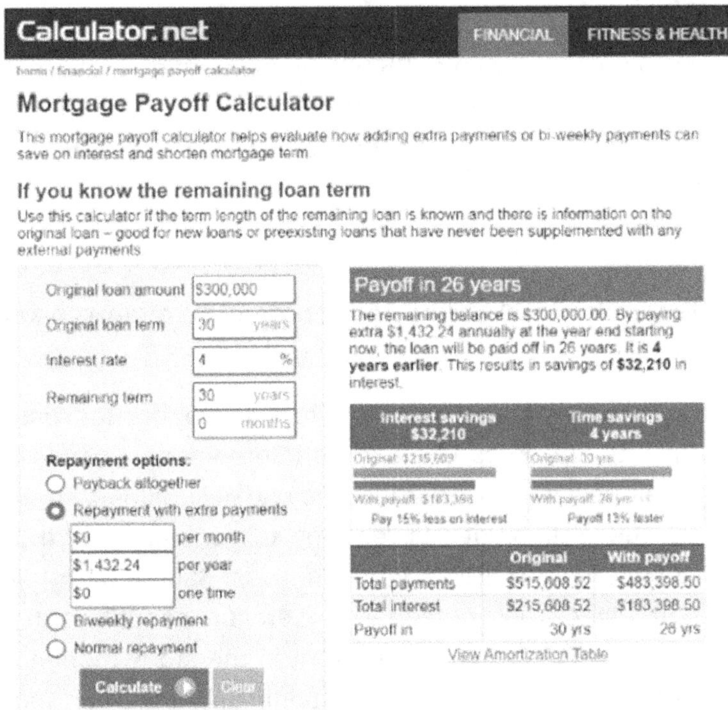

Exhibit 8.10 Mortgage Payoff Calculator Results

On the website page, she enters her mortgage loan amount of $300,000 in the original loan amount field, her mortgage loan payback period of 30 years in the original loan term field, her mortgage loan interest rate at 4% in the interest rate field and her remaining years to pay off the loan in the remaining term field, which is 30 years in this case. In the webpage Repayment Options section, Kim selects the **Repayment with extra payment** option, enters the one extra payment amount of $1,432.24, then clicks on the **Calculate** button. The webpage refreshes with the results. The one extra payment reduces the loan payback period by four years. Exhibit 8.10 is a screenshot of the webpage results.

Quick Exercise 8.2

You have a personal loan of $5,000 with an interest rate of 8%, a payback period of 6 years, and a monthly payment amount of $87.67. What is the payback period after applying an extra payment amount of $100 per month?

Income Generation and Value Appreciation Through the Use of Liabilities

Just as liabilities can be a foe to your effort for financial independence, they also can be a friend. Some people would argue you can't obtain mass wealth without the use of liabilities. I believe a delicate balance of liabilities is required to generate wealth at an accelerated pace. For example, you can invest $300 a month in the stock market using your personal brokerage account, option A. Option B, you can invest $10,010 upfront in the stock market using your personal brokerage account by obtaining a three-year personal loan for $10,010 with an interest rate of 5% and a monthly payment of $300. Let's assume your investment return in the three-year period is 10% in year 1, -2% in year 2, and 20% in year 3. Take a look at both option outcomes in Exhibit 8.11.

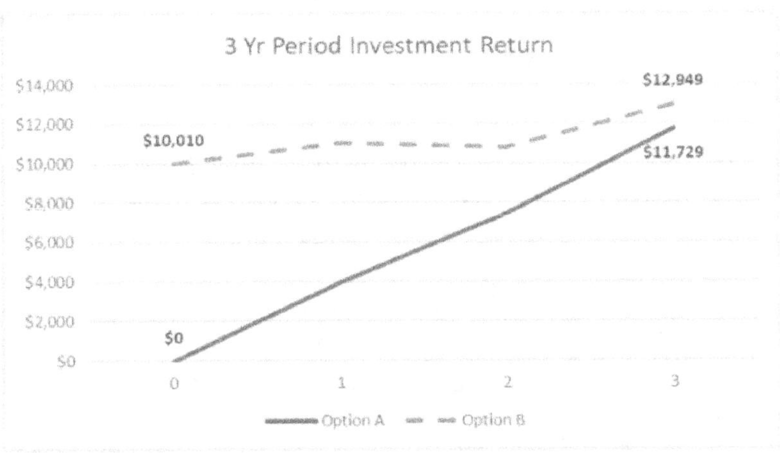

Exhibit 8.11 Options Investment Return

At the end of year 3, option B's investment return is $1,200 greater than option A's due to option B's large investment amount upfront in year 0. Option A's investment return aggressively grew over time due to the monthly $300 investment plus the yearly investment return. While each option costs you $300 per month whether in a loan payment or an investment contribution, option B produces the greatest result given the effects of investing a large lump sum of money upfront with time. When you don't have a large lump sum of money available, the usage of debt (a liability) can yield superior results than the alternative option, option A. The power of compounding interest is in full swing when there's a large sum of money and plenty of time. You'll learn more about compounding interest in Chapter 10.

The risk of losing money due to investment risks and uncertainties is possible; however, I would encourage you to ponder the decision from this perspective. Let's say you didn't invest the $300 a month but elected to spend it on hobbies or entertainment. You essentially lost the $300 each month since you didn't save the money or spend the money on necessities. The decision to spend the $300 a month on hobbies or entertainment results in a guaranteed total loss of $300, while the decision to invest the $300 a month comes with an outcome of total loss, some loss, small gains, or massive gains.

Tip: *There is always an opportunity for money to regain its losses over time when the money is invested. When money is spent on nonessential goods or services, the money is gone.*

Are you concerned about the inability to pay the loan payment each month? The concern is fair, but if you're comfortable enough to spend the $300 each month on hobbies or entertainment, then the $300 monthly loan payment isn't a financial problem. In a situation where you've taken out the loan, but after a year or more you're unable to make the payments, you have the option to sell your investment. This decision allows you to pay off the remaining loan balance and potentially keep some of your investment gains, so still a winwin. Investing $300 a month is a smart financial move. Using the $300 a month to borrow a lump sum of money to invest is a next level financial savvy move. I would be careless if I didn't mention other opportunities to use borrowed money for investing such as real estate, tax liens, artwork, business ventures, etc. The financing of an investment opportunity occurs in three ways: 1. Your money, 2. Raising money from people or 3. Borrowing money from lenders.

Quick Exercise Answers

1. 80.5 months (6.7

Rank	Debt	Payoff Period
1	Credit Card	30 months
2	Line of Credit	10.5 months
3	Student Loan	40 months
	Total	80.5 months

With the monthly payment of $473.22, the credit card balance is paid off in 30 months. In the same timeframe, the line of credit balance decreases to $5,360.98 given the $50 minimum monthly payments and the student loan balance shrinks to $30,525.08 due to its fixed monthly payment of $276.78. After the credit card is paid off, its monthly payment of $523.22 is applied to the line of credit monthly payment. As a result, the line of credit balance is paid off in 10.5 months. After the payoff of the line of credit, the remaining balance on the student loan is $29,236.30. With the monthly payment of $800, the student loan balance is paid off in 40 months.

2. 29 months

   Enter into a financial calculator: PV $5,000, Payment - $187.67, Interest Rate 8%, then compute Periods.

Chapter Test

1. With a credit card balance of $12,000, an interest rate of 19%, and minimum payment amount of $100, if you apply a $500 payment each month, how many months until the credit card is paid off?

2. You have an auto loan for $18,000 with an interest rate of 3%, a payback period of six years, and a monthly payment of $372.86. If you apply an additional $140 each month to month payment, how many years does it take to pay off the auto loan?

Chapter Test Answers

1. 30 months

    Enter into the financial calculator: PV $12,000, Interest Rate% 19, Payment -$500, then compute Period.

2. 3 years

    Enter into the financial calculator: PV $18,000, Interest Rate% 3, Payment -$512.86, then compute Period 36.77.

    37 months ÷ 12 = 3.08 equivalent to 3 years

Chapter 9

The Invisible Rat: Inflation

In 2020, something happened that only occurs in movies, like Outbreak in 1995 and Contagion in 2011. The world experienced a pandemic where a virus known as COVID spread rapidly throughout the globe at an accelerated pace. So much so that the global economies came to a screeching halt. For two months, restaurants, airlines, cruises, movie theaters, dry cleaners, barbershops, and nonessential stores shut down to slow down the rapid spread of the virus. Some of these industries remain hindered by reopening restrictions, limiting operations and employment for the next 18 months. 69 million people were laid off or furloughed in 2020 alone. To avert the failure of world economies, mass government stimulus programs were established for individuals, businesses, and capital markets. Since people couldn't spend their money on experiences, services, or inperson purchases, online buying escalated to unbelievable heights. The intermediate results of these events became supply chain and logistic nightmares for companies to restart and rescale their operations. Multiple industries seized the opportunity to exploit surge pricing. End result: the world economies had massive inflation. Exhibit 9.1 illustrates inflation during the pandemic for the U.S.

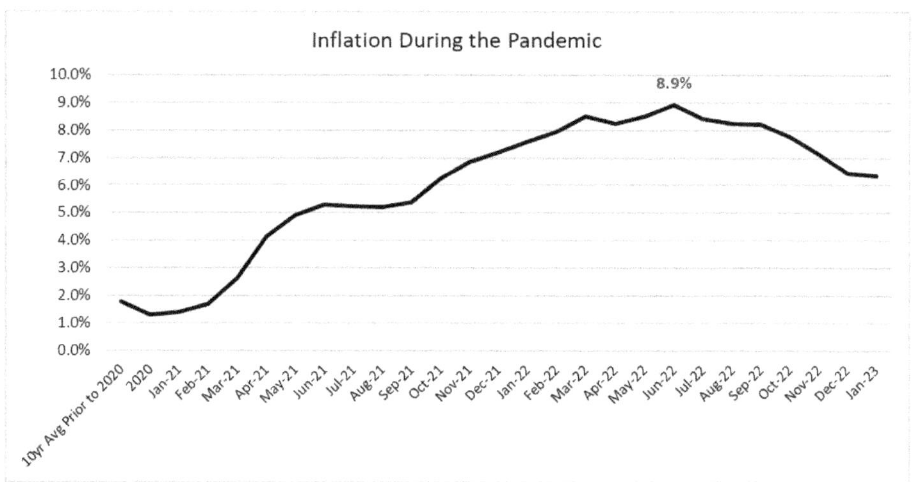

Exhibit 9.1 Inflation During the COVID Pandemic

Inflation was considered temporary by most economists and safeguards of the economies as inflation rose early in 2021. They learned quickly that the massive inflation wasn't temporary; therefore, prudent actions were taken by the U.S. Federal Reserve to curve the U.S. inflation.

Tip: *When the cost of an item increases over time, that is inflation.*

Inflation Impacts Your Purchase Power

Before this inflationary period occurred, no one born in the late 80s, now adults, experienced inflation. It was a subject matter harped on by high school economic teachers of its significance but hadn't been taken seriously given its past decade of irrelevance. During the COVID pandemic period, inflation became the Grinch that stole Christmas. But, instead of a one-time event during the year, inflation stole money month after month. Everyday necessities became luxuries. Food at grocery stores increased 13% in a year period. Fast food cost 8% more than a year prior. Transportation services to commute to work increased 16% more. Inflation was ridiculous. A guilty pleasure such as a Little Debbie Honey Bun price went from $0.50 to $2.50. The price of a Big Kahuna sub at New Jersey Mike's rose from $8 to $20. A McDonald's $5 combo burger was far in the distance. If people weren't burdened by the new cost of necessities, they sought to get out of the house and travel, since everyone had cabin fever for over a year. Unfortunately, the cost of airline tickets soared to 28% vs. its prior year's cost, dampening that enjoyment.

Inflation Eats Away at Your Cash

A savings account is considered the safest place for cash. The cash is secured away from thieves and accidental home fires. But, in a high-inflation environment, keeping cash in a savings account is

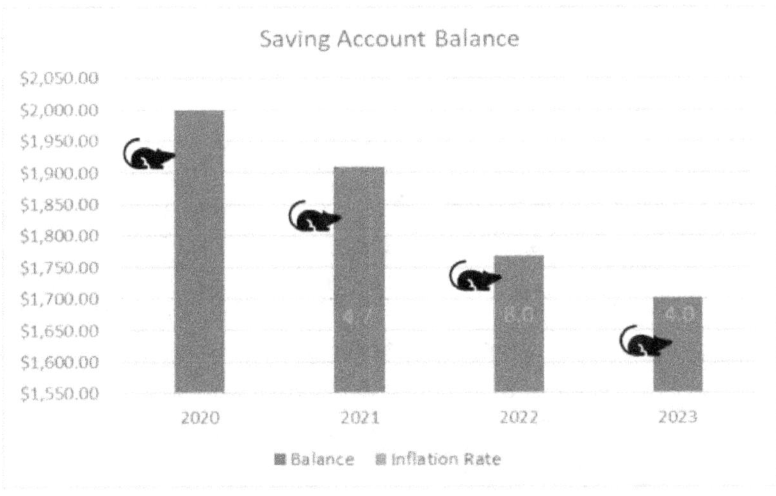

Exhibit 9.2 Saving Account Erosion

equivalent to letting a rat in a safe full of cheese (money). Do you expect the same amount of cheese to remain after the rat has spent time in the safe? The rat is inflation. Exhibit 9.2 shows how much the rat has eaten of your savings cash since 2020, if you had $2,000 in your savings account. Over the three-year period, 2021 through 2023, the rat has eaten $300 from your savings account. While your savings account balance still displays $2,000, the cash is worth $1,700 because the price of goods and services has gone up over the years. Remember in Chapter 3, you learned about your savings cash generating income (interest) through purchases of T-Bills, which are risk-free assets. The interest rate on a T-bill is also referred to as the nominal rate. By subtracting the inflation rate from the nominal rate, you end up with the real rate. Check out Exhibit 9.3 table of nominal, inflation, and real rates.

Years	Nominal Rate	Inflation Rate	Real Rate
2021	0.1%	4.7%	-4.60%
2022	2.8%	8.0%	-5.20%
2023	5.0%	4.0%	1.00%

Exhibit 9.3 Nominal, Inflation, and Real Rates

Tip: *Nominal rate is the gross interest rate, while the real rate is the net interest rate after taking into account the inflation rate.*

Notice the real rates for 2021 and 2022 were negative. The purchase of T-Bills in an inflationary environment provides you with some protection against inflation. If you invested your savings account cash of $2,000 in a one-year T-Bill from 2021 through 2023, your savings account balance would look different than Exhibit 9.2 results. Here is a comparison of the savings account balance with no T-Bill purchase vs. T-Bill purchase in Exhibit 9.4. The numbers inside each column represent the real rate. The T-Bill purchased in 2022 absorbed some of inflation's pain that year, while the T-Bill purchased in 2023 increased the savings balance due to the 1% real rate.

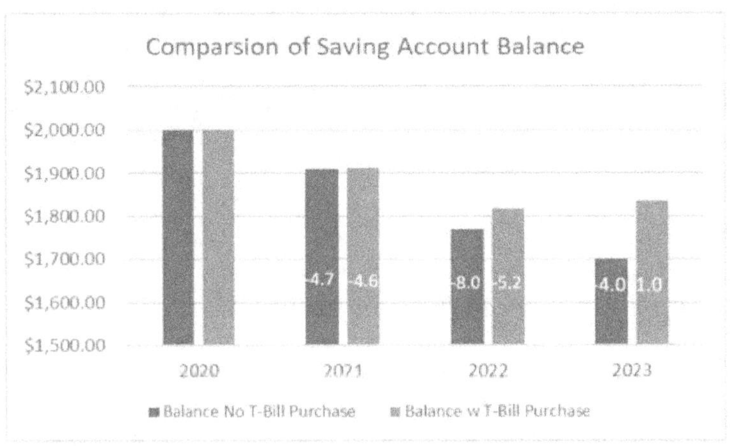

Exhibit 9.4 No T-Bill Purchase vs T-Bill Purchase

While the interest rates on T-Bills may seem insignificant, in the grand scheme of things, they are a powerful weapon in the battle against inflation. Your savings account balance isn't the only item impacted by inflation.

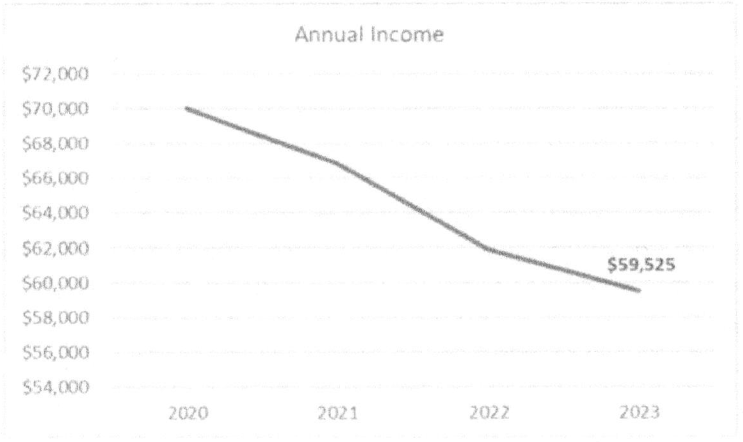

Exhibit 9.5 Annual Income Deterioration

Your annual income is diminished by the pesty rat as well. See the ramifications of your income diminishment since 2020 if you haven't switched jobs, or received a promotion or a merited raise in Exhibit 9.5. Over the three-year period, the value of your income decreased by 15% because of the rising cost of goods and services.

Tip: *Your employer increases its services' or goods' prices to combat inflation. Shouldn't your services to your employer cost more as well?*

Who Controls the Interest Rate on T-Bills

In the U.S., the Federal Reserve controls treasury rates through a few mechanics. The primary mechanic is setting the federal fund rate, FED fund rate. The FED fund rate is consistently adjusted by the Federal Reserve to maintain price stability thus attempting to keep inflation at a reasonable rate of 2%. Given the FED fund rate is used by banks as a benchmark to set borrowing rates for credit products such as mortgages, loans, credit cards, and line of credits, lowering the federal fund rate incentivizes banks to lend more to borrowers. Borrowers are more willing to borrow money from banks since rates are favorable (lower). The borrowed money is channeled into the purchase of goods and services, thereby stimulating economic activity. The Federal Reserve lowers the Fed fund rate to prevent an economic recession or to jumpstart the economy from a recession. In these circumstances, the inflation rate is lower than its 2% target.

When inflation is high and above the target rate, the Federal Reserve raises the FED fund rate. Consequently, the rates on T-Bills increase as displayed in Exhibit 9.3: nominal rates. The rise of the FED fund rate slows down economic activity. Borrowers are reluctant to borrow money from banks due to higher bank interest rates. Banks don't have an incentive to lend money, since their deposits and capital (money) can earn a profit invested in T-Bills. The Federal Reserve achieves its objective of reining inflation back to its 2% target. Unfortunately, this achievement comes with people losing their jobs. **Moral of this chapter**—don't get comfortable with seeing your money stack up in your savings account. Put your money to work! It has a job just like you do.

Chapter Test

1. Who controls U.S. interest rates?
    a. U.S. Congress
    b. U.S. President
    c. U.S. Federal Reserve
    d. U.S. Military

2. If the one-year T-Bill interest rate is 2.5% and the inflation rate is 2.3%. What is the real rate?
    a. 1.0%
    b. 0.2%
    c. 5.8%
    d. 0.5%

3. When the cost of an item increases over time, that is inflation.
    a. True
    b. False

4. The real rate is the net interest rate after taking into account only the nominal rate.
    a. True
    b. False

5. Nominal rate is the gross interest rate.
    a. True
    b. False

6. The U.S. Federal Reserve attempts to keep inflation at which target rate?
    a. 2%
    b. 3%
    c. 1%
    d. 5%

Chapter Test Answers

1. C (U.S. Federal Reserve)
2. B (0.2%)

   2.5% (T-Bill interest rate) – 2.3% (Inflation rate) = 0.2%

3. A (True)
4. B (False)

   The real rate is the net interest rate after taking into account the nominal rate and inflation rate.

5. A (True)
6. A (2%)

Chapter 10

How to Make Your Money Grow: Compounding Interest, Rule of 72, and Present Value

Prior to reading this book, you may have heard of compounding interest. The consensus is that compounding interest is a powerful tool that can grow your retirement funds enormously by the time you reach retirement age. Or, compounding interest has the power to create generational wealth. But, has anyone explained to you how compounding interest works?

Before I do, let's quickly cover simple interest. Let's say you have a friend named Megan. Megan asks you for $100 and says she will give you back $105 in a year. As a result, your interest on the $100 for the year is 5% ($5), which is simple interest. If Megan paid back the $100 after a year based on compounding interest quarterly, she would give you $105.09. The additional $.09 is due to Megan paying quarterly interest on interest accumulated in the previous periods. There are four periods within a year from a quarterly standpoint. The first period, you'll receive a quarterly equivalent interest on the $100, which is $1.25.

$100 (Original amount) x .0125 (5% ÷ 4) = $1.25

5% is the interest rate and four represents the quarterly basis. In the second period, you'll receive quarterly equivalent interest based on the original amount plus first period interest.

$101.25 (Original amount plus first period interest) x .0125 (5% ÷ 4) = 1.26

The third period quarterly equivalent interest is based on the original balance plus first period and second period interest.

$102.51 (Original amount plus first period interest and second interest) x .0125 (5% ÷ 4) = 1.28

The fourth and last period interest is based on the original balance plus first period, second period, and third period.

$103.79 (Original amount plus first period interest, second interest, and third period interest) x .0125 (5% ÷ 4) = $1.30.

First Period Interest	$1.25
Second Period Interest	$1.26
Third Period Interest	$1.28
Fourth Period Interest	$1.30
Original Amount	$100.00
Total Amount	$105.09

Check out the amount of money Megan would have paid you, if the $100 compounding interest was based on daily, monthly, and semi-annually in Exhibit 10.1.

Daily	$105.13
Monthly	$105.12
Semi-Annually	$105.06

Exhibit 10.1 Compounding Interest Basis

Tip: *All things equal, daily compounding interest always yields the highest returns.*

Computing the results of compounding interest is very taxing when performed manually on paper. The same financial calculator app used in Chapter 6 makes finding compounding interest results easy. For instance, you invest $500 that has a rate of return of 12% for three years on a monthly basis. Using the financial calculator app, enter the following values in Exhibit 10.2 to find the future value of $500 after three years.

Present Value	500.00
Payments	0
Future Value	
Annual Rate%	12
Periods	36
Compounding	Monthly

Exhibit 10.2 Find Results of Compounding Interest

Given the interest accumulates on a monthly basis, the period's value is 36 months and the compounding value is monthly. Once you have the values entered in the calculator, click the Future Value (FV) button to populate the results. In this example, the future value is $715.38.

Quick Exercise 10.1

Mark invested $5,000 into a cryptocurrency that value increased 25% on a quarterly basis for five years. What is the value of $5,000 after five years?

Time is the greatest factor when considering compounding interest powers. For instance, Jacob started investing $500 per month for 30 years at a 5% rate of return. After 15 years, Melissa started investing $1,000 per month for 15 years at an 8% rate of return. Which person has the greatest amount of money at the end of the period?

	Jacob	Melissa
Present Value	$0	$0
Payments	$500.00	$1,000.00
Future Value	$416,129	$346,038
Annual Rate%	5	8
Periods	360	180
Compounding	Monthly	Monthly

Despite Melissa doubling her monthly investment amount in comparison to Jacob's and her annual rate 50% greater than Jacob's annual rate, her future investment amount falls short by $70,000 compared to Jacob's.

Tip: *Time is a virtue in life as well as in compounding interest, so use time wisely*

Rule of 72

I learned the Rule of 72 during my junior year of college interning for Primerica, the Life Insurance company. Little did I know this principle would stick with me. Perhaps you have a desire to double your money in three years; do you know the rate of return required to make it happen? How would you find the rate of return? The Rule of 72 answers both questions with simple math. You divide 72 by the number of years that you want your money to double. To double your investment in three years, you need an annual return rate of 24%.

$$72 \div 3 \text{ (Number of Years)} = 24\%$$

What if you were offered an opportunity to invest your money with an annual return rate of 12%? How would you determine the number of years required for your money to double? Divide 72 by the annual return rate.

$$72 \div 12 \text{ (Annual Return Rate)} = 6 \text{ years}$$

The Rule of 72 is easy to remember, plus it helps you assess risk and reward dilemmas from a time perspective. Investment A at 15% return is less risky than Investment B at 30% return. Investment A doubles your money in 4.8 years, while Investment B doubles your money in 2.4 years. Are you willing to take on the additional risk with Investment B for a shorter period to double your money?

Quick Exercise 10.2

Your 401k balance annual growth rate is 8%. How many years are required for your money to double?

This principle is applicable outside of the investment world as well. For example, your business revenue is growing annually by 10%. Using the Rule of 72, you can determine how many years it would take for your revenue to double. Or what growth rate would have your revenue double in four years?

Quick Exercise 10.3

If your business profit's annual growth rate of 32% continues, how many years does it take to double your profits?

Present Value / Future Value

Earlier in this chapter, you used the financial calculator app to find the compounding interest future value. The tool also can find the present value of an expected future value. For instance, you plan to retire at age 65 with $4 million. You're curious to know the present value of $4 million, so you can assess the $4 million worth in today's economy since you're 20 years old right now. Using the financial calculator app, enter the values in Exhibit 10.3

Present Value	
Payments	0
Future Value	$4,000,000
Annual Rate%	2
Periods	540
Compounding	Monthly

Exhibit 10.3 Finding the Present Value of $4 million

Notice that an educated assumption is made on the annual rate. The 2% represents the target inflation rate by the Federal Reserve and economists. Also, U.S. history has approved that the U.S. inflation hovers around 2%. The difference between your retirement age and current age in years is converted to months for the period's value. Select the Present Value (PV) button on the calculator to display the answer. In this case, the present value is $1,627,497.

Quick Exercise 10.4

You desire a future salary of $350,000 10 years from now. What is the present value of the future salary when compounding on a quarterly basis and the annual rate is 2.5%?

From ensuring your desired annual income keeps up with inflation to assessing your retirement financial needs, compounding interest and the rule of 72 have the capability to change your life when applied in a rational and thoughtful manner.

Quick Exercise Answers

1. $16,809.27

Present Value	$5,000.00
Payments	0
Future Value	**$16,809.27**
Annual Rate%	25
Periods	20
Compounding	Quarterly

2. 9 years

   72 ÷ 8 (Rate of Return) = 9

3. 2.25 years

   72 ÷ 32 (Growth Rate) = 2.25 years

4. $272,792

Present Value	$272,279
Payments	0
Future Value	$350,000
Annual Rate%	2.5
Periods	40
Compounding	Quarterly

Chapter Test

1. You decide to invest $700 a month for 20 years. Assuming your rate of return is 10% every month, how much money do you have after 20 years?
    a. $168,000
    b. $250,100
    c. $410,600
    d. $531,558
2. In nine years, you would like your initial investment to double. What is the annual return rate required?
    a. 5%
    b. 10%
    c. 8%
    d. 3%
3. Malcolm started investing $400 per month for 5 years at a 50% rate of return. Nicole started investing $1,000 per month for 10 years at a 20% rate of return. Which person has the greatest amount of money at the end of the period?
    a. Malcolm
    b. Nicole
4. You're curious to know the future value of $3 million five years from now. The annual rate is 3% and compounding is monthly.
5. Twenty-seven years from now, you desire your IRA account to have $8 million. What is the present value of the $8 million assuming an annual rate of 2% and compounding monthly?
6. Which compounding basis yields the highest return, if all other factors are equal?
    a. Monthly
    b. Quarterly
    c. Daily
    d. Annually
    e. Semi-Annually

Chapter Test Answers

1. D ($531,558)

Present Value	$0
Payments	$-700
Future Value	**$531,558**
Annual Rate%	10
Periods	240
Compounding	Monthly

2. C (8%)

$72 \div 9$ (years) $= 8$

3. B (Nicole)

	Malcom	Nicole
Present Value	$0	$0
Payments	$400.00	$1,000.00
Future Value	**$101,572**	**$376,096**
Annual Rate%	50	20
Periods	60	120
Compounding	Monthly	Monthly

4. $3,484,850

Present Value	$3,000,000
Payments	$0
Future Value	**$3,484,850**
Annual Rate%	3
Periods	60
Compounding	Monthly

5. $4,664,082

Present Value	**$4,664,082**
Payments	$0
Future Value	$8,000,000
Annual Rate%	2
Periods	324
Compounding	Monthly

6. C (Daily)

Chapter 11

How to Establish and Advance Your Credit

Having good credit can make life easier than you'll ever realized. You may volunteer frequently at a shelter, lead a church committee, or mentor a young teen. Unfortunately, those good deeds and strong character traits don't reflect in your credit score. When you think of credit, think of credibility. Your creditworthiness is a representation of you. Some processes and systems determine who you are as a person based on your credit score. Your credit score is another data point to assess whether you are a good candidate for a job opportunity, a worthy borrower for a loan, or ideal applicant for an apartment lease. There are three levels of credibility as it pertains to credit:

1. No Credibility = No Credit
2. Bad Credibility = Bad Credit
3. Good Credibility = Good Credit

Everyone starts with no credibility, so there is no shame there. At some point in time, you must begin establishing credit. If you don't, your no credibility becomes parity with bad credibility. Your credit is your non-public reputation. Protect it as you would protect the king on the chessboard.

Ways to Establish Credit

Typically, you receive your first opportunity to obtain credit at the age of 18 on college campuses. Banks and credit companies offer credit card signups to young adults among other services. From the banks' and credit companies' perspectives, young adults at that point are untapped new customers for a range of products: student loans, checking accounts, savings accounts, and credit cards. If you aren't enrolled in college, the opportunity arises as you open a checking account to directly deposit your work paycheck.

Tip: *Take a proactive approach to establish credit as soon as possible. Don't wait until you need to borrow money to be concerned about your credit.*

Unknown to most people, you don't have to wait until you're 18 years old to establish credit. Your parents can start your credit journey early by adding you as an authorized user on their credit card. As a result, you can build credit history and time, which are factors in determining your credit score. The decision to be added to your parents' credit card doesn't come without risk. If your parents miss a payment on the credit card or are late making a payment on the credit card, your credit takes a negative hit. Before asking to be added to your parents' credit card, have a conversation with your parents on the matter. Inquire on the number of times they have missed a payment on their credit card in the last two years. Do they constantly use more than 40% of their credit card limit? If the answer is more than twice for the first question and yes for the second question, then you may want to reconsider asking to be added as an authorized user. In a respectful matter, inquire whether your parents' credit score is considered bad, average, good, or excellent. If the answer is bad or average, you're better off waiting to have your credit card. While this guidance sounds harsh, managing your credit can't be taken lightly.

Here are a few precautions that you can take after being added as an authorized user to your parents' credit card:

1. Ask for the credit card monthly payment due date, then track the due date to remind your parents of the payment.
2. Limit your authorized user to one of your parents' credit cards.

Another option available to establish credit is to open a secured credit card once you're 18 years old. This decision requires you to give the credit card provider between $200 to $300 to secure the credit card. The money is applied to your credit card as the credit limit; therefore, you can't spend more than $200 to $300.

Tip: *Use your secured credit card for small purchases such as gas for your car or lunch for work, so the purchases are not difficult to pay off.*

To ensure your credit card activity isn't a deterrent to increasing your credit score, your credit card period ending balance shouldn't exceed 20% of the credit card limit. This concept is known as the credit utilization rate. For example, if your secured credit card has a credit limit of $200 and you practice the 20% credit utilization rate restriction, then your credit card's monthly ending balance can't exceed $20.

Tip: *Credit utilization rate indicates how much of the credit card limit you used in percentage terms.*

Credit Utilization Rate: Credit Card Outstanding Balance ÷ Credit Card Limit

Quick Exercise 11.1

Your secured credit card has a credit limit of $500. If you restrict your credit card activity to a credit utilization rate of 20%, your month ending balance can't exceed how much?

After a year of on-time payments, your credit card provider returns the $200 to $300 back to you. Your credit card becomes unsecured with a credit limit. Over time your credit limit increases with the continuation of on-time payments, credit utilization rate under 25%, and income growth.

How Your FICO (Credit Score) is Determined

There are six factors that affect your credit score. These factors are listed below on their relative importance in influencing your credit score:

1. Payment History
2. Credit Card Usage
3. Derogatory Marks
4. Credit Age
5. Total Accounts
6. Hard Inquiries

Payment History

For good reason, payment history is number 1 in terms of impact on your credit score. Paying back what you have borrowed is core to the credit concept. You start with 100% payment history, full credibility. There is no doubt that you will pay back what you owe.

Every time you miss a payment or make a late payment, you chip away at the full (100%) credibility. The ramifications of a missed or late payment are different depending on the credit product. There is no leeway for missing a payment or being late on a payment for revolving credit, such as credit cards and line of credit. The negative hit to your credit happens the next day after missing the payment due date. For non-revolving credit such as term loans, mortgages, student loans and auto loans, you have 30 days from the payment due date before a negative consequence occurs to your credit. I didn't call out the different ramifications for you to juggle the importance of payment between revolving credit vs. non-revolving credit. Your best approach is to pay all your bills and debts on time, every time.

Tip: *Know your debts' due dates as well as you know your cell phone number. If you're concerned about remembering the due dates, then you have too many debts. Remember Herm Edwards' philosophy—one of everything. Given the penalty is high for a missed credit card payment, one credit card is enough.*

The ranking of payment history as the number 1 factor isn't due to qualitative reasons. Your payment history represents 35% of the credit score calculation, which is the highest percentage factor within the credit score model.

Credit Card Usage

Think of your credit card usage from a grading scale perspective. The higher the usage rate, the poorer the grade. Exhibit 11.1. is a visual of the grading scale.

Years	Status
0% – 9%	Excellent
10% – 29%	Good
30% – 49%	Fair
>50%	Needs Work

Exhibit 11.1 Credit Card Usage Grade Scale[12]

You may be asking yourself, what is the purpose of having a credit card if my credit score is penalized for using too much of the credit card? While the concept may seem counterintuitive, a high usage rate of your credit card is considered an indicator that a borrower is in distress. A distressed borrower doesn't have enough cash coming in to pay for bills or purchases, thus relying on the credit card. Remember, your credit card usage rate is finalized at the month end date; therefore, you can make purchases that account for a sizable amount of the credit card limit as long as you pay down the credit card balance to a decent usage rate before the month end date. Credit card providers reward low usage rates, such as below 25%, with increases to your credit card limit. From a credit card provider's perspective, a low usage rate is an indicator that the borrower isn't dependent on the credit card limit; thus, they have adequate cash to pay for bills and purchases. An independent borrower is more likely to pay off the balance on the credit card.

Tip: *Credit card usage rate accounts for 30% of the credit score calculation, which is the second-highest percentage within the credit score model.*

Derogatory Marks

The lease on you and your roommate's apartment expires. The apartment manager assesses a $75 fee for unusual damages to the apartment. Your roommate agrees to pay the $75 fee. After multiple attempts to have you and your roommate pay the $75 balance, the apartment manager stops calling. As your background check is running for a separate apartment with another apartment complex, you're informed a derogatory mark is on your credit report for the unpaid bill at your prior apartment complex. A derogatory mark on your credit occurs when you don't pay an outstanding bill over a period of time. The company that you own the bill to decides you won't pay the bill. As a result, the company writes off the outstanding bill as a loss, and then reports your outstanding bill to the credit bureau. The credit bureau places the outstanding bill on your credit as a derogatory mark.

To have the mark removed from your credit report, you must pay the outstanding bill. Ensure that you obtain a receipt of the bill paid in full, then request the company to have the credit bureau remove the mark from your credit report. If the company doesn't take the requested action, you can request the removal of the mark with the credit bureau. Provide the receipt of the bill paid in full as proof of payment.

Tip: *A derogatory mark falls off your credit report after 7 to 10 years regardless if you paid the outstanding bill.*

If a derogatory mark is incorrect or due to fraudulent activity, you can dispute the mark with credit reporting companies like Experian, Equifax, and (or) Transunion. You can avoid such blemishes on your credit report by always paying what you owe no matter the amount. When sharing responsibility with someone that involves signing contracts, you are just as responsible for any unpaid fees, services, and damages. Think hard and think twice when you decide to share credit responsibility with someone.

Credit Age

Age isn't simply a number when it comes to your credit. Obtaining access to credit as soon as possible is your best action to having this factor trending upward in your favor. The determination of your credit age is based on the collective average time of all open credit accounts; therefore, opening a new credit account affects your existing credit age. For example, your credit card has been open for 7 years. You decide to obtain an auto loan to purchase a car. As a result, your credit age declines from 7 years to 3.5 years.

Credit Age: Sum the age of all credits ÷ number of credits

Quick Exercise 11.2

Status	Credit	Credit Age
Existing	Credit Card	11 years 6 months
Existing	Student Loan	12 years 2 months
Existing	Auto Loan	3 years 4 months
Existing	Personal Loan	1 year
New	Mortgage	0

Before obtaining a mortgage for a house, your credit age is 8 years and 3 months. What is your credit age after obtaining a mortgage for a house?

Tip: *Try to avoid closing your long tender credit accounts as much as possible. Closing an older credit account damages your credit age and hurts your credit score.*

Considering only Quick Exercise 11.2 existing credit accounts, if the credit card account closes, the credit age drops 35% to 5 years and 5 months. The credit age status went from Good to Fair based on the Credit Age Grade Scale in Exhibit 11.3.

Years	Status
0 – 4	Need Work
5 – 6	Fair
7 – 8	Good
9+	Excellent

Exhibit 11.3 Credit Age Grade Scale[13]

Total Accounts

The accumulation of multiple credit accounts comes in time; there's no point in rushing to open different credit account types. The impact of total accounts is minimal toward your credit score. At this point of the credit section, you know your first credit account should be a credit card. Your next credit account could be a student loan, auto loan, or mortgage loan depending on your path in life. No matter the number of accounts, honor the responsibility to keep each account in good standing.

Tip: *Once your credit score is in a good place and you have a few years on your credit card account, contact your credit card provider. Ask for a reduction on your credit card interest rate. You have earned it! Emphasize that you want to keep the same credit card (credit account) but have the interest rate lower. You don't want the provider* mistakenly closing the account; subsequently, opening a new account with a lower interest rate.

Hard Inquiries

When opening a credit account such as a credit card, student loan, auto loan, or mortgage loan, you are subject to a hard inquiry, which is a comprehensive review of your credit profile and history by the credit provider. Too many hard inquiries within a 24-month time span hurt your credit score. Credit providers interpret numerous hard inquiries as a person who's desperate for credit or settled with new credit obligations. A hard inquiry can stay on your credit for 24 months before the inquiry falls off. Exhibit 11.4 is a table of the hard inquiry grade scale. Without getting into the details of a soft inquiry, just know a soft inquiry does not impact your credit score, so no worries when an account opening requires a soft inquiry. Common soft inquiries on your credit are pre-approval offers and apartment leases.

Hard Inquiry	Status
5+	Need Work
4 - 5	Fair
1 - 2	Good
0	Excellent

Exhibit 11.4 Hard Inquiry Grade Scale[14]

Tip: *Before opening any account, ask whether the account opening requires a hard inquiry to your credit.*

Learn About Your Credit Score and Report with Free Online Services

Knowing is only half the battle; acting is the other half. You can take action on managing your credit by tracking your credit score. There are a few avenues to track your credit score. If you have a checking or savings account, your bank provides your credit score through its bank mobile application or website. Log in to the application or website to obtain your credit score. Some banks display your credit score history in a nice line chart, so you can observe the changes in your credit score over the last 12 months.

Another resource for **tracking your credit score is creditkarma.com.** It offers your credit score from two credit bureaus:

Transunion and Equifax. For each credit bureau's credit score, Credit Karma evaluates your performance in the credit factors: Payment History, Credit Card Usage, Derogatory Marks, Total Accounts, and Hard Inquiries. Perhaps your credit card usage rose to 37% in the current month due to unexpected expenses. Credit Karma displays the impact that the higher credit card usage rate has on your credit score for that month by the two credit bureaus. This assessment occurs for all the credit factors mentioned earlier. In addition to your credit scores, you can obtain a free annual credit report from Credit Karma, so you can stay informed of any changes in your credit history and monitor any potential signs of identity theft or fraud.

Tip: *Experian.com also offers your annual credit report for free.*

Benefits of Good Credit

You have options! With many options comes power (leverage) in financial decision-making. Options give you the capability to negotiate, walk away, and ponder a financial decision on your terms. The path to obtaining these financial options is through good credit and financial discipline. Besides increase financing options, good credit comes with favorable interest rates thus a lower borrowing cost (monthly expense). The difference between a 2% interest rate vs. 5% interest rate can result in saving thousands of dollars. Good credit also impacts your employment opportunities in a meaningful way. Perceiving someone with good credit as having strong decision-making skills and high integrity is not a far reach. Your credit score says more than whether you deserve a certain level of interest rate. Your credit is a representation of your character, good or bad.

Quick Exercise Answers

1. $100

$500 (Credit Card Limit) x 20% (Utilization Rate) = $100 (Credit Card Balance)

2. 5 years and 6 months

28 (numbers of credit years) ÷ 5 (number of credit accounts = 5.6

Chapter Test

1. Select the item that does not require a hard inquiry on your credit:
    a. Credit Card
    b. Apartment Lease
    c. Mortgage Loan
    d. Line of Credit
2. With a credit card balance of $1,250 and a credit card limit of $4,000, what is your credit card utilization rate?
    a. 40.00%
    b. 25.00%
    c. 31.25%
    d. 17.50%
3. Which factor has the highest impact on your credit score?
    a. Credit Card Usage
    b. Payment History
    c. Total Accounts
    d. Hard Inquiries
4. A derogatory mark on your credit occurs when you don't pay an outstanding bill over a period of time.
    a. True
    b. False

Chapter Test Answers

1. B (Apartment Lease)
2. C (31.25%)

   $1,250 (Credit Card Balance) ÷ $4,000 (Credit Card Limit) = 31.25%

3. B (Payment History)
4. A (True)

Final Thoughts

Thank you for taking the time to start and finish the book. I am far from one of the world's best writers, so your ability to stick through the material and keep an open mind says a lot about your character as well as your conviction to better yourself financially. The tips, skills, and lessons learned from this book are a starting point in your journey of financial stability and prosperity. Don't waste time. Take action immediately. Continue your journey by implementing what you have learned. From creating a spending plan, starting emergency savings, opening a treasury direct account, investing in your 401k (IRA), and eliminating excess debt to establishing credit, there are numerous actions you can take now. Your biggest obstacle will be fear. Don't be afraid to fail. You will make mistakes, but mistakes are growing pains. Mistakes are fixable; regrets aren't.

It's a long journey. As with any journey, there are checkpoints. While you are implementing some of the actions mentioned earlier, your first checkpoint is the book Rich Dad Poor Dad by Robert T. Kiyosaki. This book has been monumental in shaping my financial principles and position.

At 25 years old, I reread Rich Dad Poor Dad since my early years as a teenager. At the time, I was working as a capital market analyst supporting the operation of asset back finance where mid-size corporations to large institutions borrowed money to make money. I realized that I fell into the trap of working hard for money instead of letting money work hard for me. Given my finance knowledge, good credit, and boldness, I took out an unsecured personal loan of $12,000 with a three-year repayment plan. Half of the money, $6,000, I invested in my parents' start-up trucking company, while the remaining $6,000 served as a cash cushion for making the monthly payment of $365. I took a calculated risk on my ability to increase my annual salary to afford the loan's monthly payment before the cash cushion was depleted in 16 months. I also anticipated that my investment in the trucking company would increase in value and provide annual income through profit distributions. The profit distributions would be used to make the loan's monthly payment and to invest into the stock market. Ultimately, I bet that my investments could generate an investment return rate greater than the loan's 6% borrowing cost (interest rate). It's safe to say that the decision panned out well. I paid off the loan on time, then repeated the process by taking out a bigger size loan, since I could afford it with my new job.

As you are inspired to make money work for you from Rich Dad Poor Dad, your next checkpoint equips you with the knowledge and skills to do so: The Five Rules for Successful Stock Investing by Pat Dorsey. This book was a part of my Financial Analyst course curriculum in my junior year of undergrad studies for finance majors. Another book that puts into perspective the path to obtaining wealth is Millionaire Next Door by Dr. Thomas J. Stanley, which is your third checkpoint. After reading this book, you will walk away with the mindset, "The broke stays broke by acting rich, while the rich stay rich by acting broke." Your final checkpoint that I must omit is a doozy: The Intelligent Investor by Benjamin Graham, Warren Buffet's greatest influencer. Despite being published 74 years ago, the investment strategies presented in this book remain effective and relevant today.

ENDNOTES

1. Annuity.org. "47+ Fascinating Financial Literacy Statistics in 2023." Last modified November 15, 2023. https://www.annuity.org/financial-literacy/financial-literacy-statistics/.

2. Ssa.gov. "Supplemental Security Income" https://www.ssa.gov/ssi#:~:text=Supplemental%20Security%20Income%20(SSI)%20(,resources%20below%20specific%20financial%20limits.

3. "North Carolina Federal Salary Paycheck Calculator Results" https://www.paycheckcity.com/calculator/salary/north-carolina/result.

4. "States with the Lowest Taxes and the Highest Taxes." Last Modified December 1, 2022. https://turbotax.intuit.com/tax-tips/fun-facts/states-with-the-highest-and-lowest-taxes/L6HPAVqSF.

5. "67 percent of private industry workers had access to retirement plans in 2020." March 1, 2021. https://www.bls.gov/opub/ted/2021/67-percent-of-private-industry-workers-had-access-to-retirement-plans-in-2020.htm

6. Bankrate.com. "8 ways to take penalty-free withdrawals from your IRA or 401(k)." October 16, 2023. https://www.bankrate.com/retirement/ways-to-take-penalty-free-withdrawals-from-ira-or-401k/

7. Schwab.com. "Traditional IRA Withdrawal Rules".
    https://www.schwab.com/ira/traditional-ira/withdrawal-rules

8. Finance.yahoo.com." U.S. consumers have spent more than $1
    trillion saved up during the pandemic." January 3, 2023.
    https://finance.yahoo.com/news/consumer-savings-spending-
    pandemic-economy-141619694.html

9. Statista.com. "Major foreign holders of United States treasury
    securities as of July 2023." July 2023.
    https://www.statista.com/statistics/246420/major-foreign-
    holders-of-us-treasury-debt/

10. Forbes.com. "5 Reasons Why 80% Of Retired NFL Players Go
    Broke." February 9, 2015.
    https://www.forbes.com/sites/leighsteinberg/2015/02/09/5-
    reasons-why-80-of-retired-nfl-players-go-
    broke/?sh=7905f0d978cc

11. Calculator.net. Mortgage Payoff Calculator
    https://www.calculator.net/mortgage-payoff-calculator.html

12. Creditkarma.com Credit Card Usage Ratings
    https://www.creditkarma.com/credit-health/factors/equifax/ccu

13. Creditkarma.com Credit Age Ratings
    https://www.creditkarma.com/credit-health/factors/equifax/aoh

14. Creditkarma.com Hard Inquiries Ratings
    https://www.creditkarma.com/credit-health/factors/equifax/inq